Who Poisoned Mary Dean?

Also by Maurie Garland
and Brolga Publishing:

The Trials of Isabella Mary Kelly
The Swiss Swagman (Editor)
Jimmy Governor: Blood on the Tracks
Horace Dean: A Pocketful of Lies

Published by Brolga Publishing Pty Ltd
ABN 46 063 962 443

PO Box 452
Torquay Victoria 3228
Australia

email: markzocchi@brolgapublishing.com.au

All rights reserved. No part of this publication may be reproduced, stored in a retrieval system or transmitted in any form or by any means electronic, mechanical, photocopying, recording or otherwise without prior permission from the publisher.

Copyright © 2019 Maurice John Garland

National Library of Australia
Cataloguing-in-Publication data
    Maurie Garland, author.
    ISBN 9780987639011 (paperback)
         9781921221149 (ebook)

 A catalogue record for this book is available from the National Library of Australia

Printed in Australia
Cover design by WorkingType Studio
Typesetting by Elly Cridland

BE PUBLISHED
Publish through a successful publisher
National Distribution to Australia & New Zealand
International Distribution to the United Kingdom
Ebooks Worldwide
Sales Representation to South East Asia
Email: markzocchi@brolgapublishing.com.au

Brolga Books by Maurie Garland

The Trials of Isabella Mary Kelly
Maurie Garland's incisive narrative, based on significant sources that have not been previously addressed by historians, unfolds her real story for the first time ... the layers have been skilfully scraped away to reveal a fresh and lively portrait of both her life and times.

- *John Ramsland*
Emeritus Professor of History, University of Newcastle

AT LAST ... the truth about the remarkable life of Isabella Mary Kelly ... a pioneer of rare quality who deserves praise.

- *Di Morrissey*

Jimmy Governor: Blood on the Tracks
Maurie Garland provides a model of historical sleuthing in this gripping account of [Jimmy] Governor's murderous rampage. The book is a superb example of the careful use of primary sources ... the result is an accurate account full of observations from people involved.

- *Sydney Morning Herald*

Horace Dean: A Pocketful of Lies
The author of this intriguing biography is to be congratulated on painstaking research into the life of [Horace] Dean.

- *Canberra Times*

This is a wonderfully rich study in 19th Century political dishonesty and skulduggery.

- *Sydney Morning Herald*

Fascinating ... [Maurie] Garland's colourful account of [Horace] Dean's life keeps the reader engrossed.

- *Trust News Australia (National Trust of Australia)*

Who Poisoned Mary Dean?

The Trial that Changed Australian Justice

Maurie Garland

Dedication

To the memory of my mother Sheila

Contents

Prologue
    Ernst Büttner on Trial ... 1

Part 1. A Marriage on Trial ... 15
    1. The First Wedding Anniversary ... 17
    2. Committal ... 27
    3. The Hanging Judge ... 45
    4. An Innocent Man ... 67
    5. The Secret Wedding ... 87

Part 2. Justice on Trial ... 101
    6. Pickpockets and Thieves ... 103
    7. Neighbours ... 127
    8. Justice Demands ... 139
    9. A Bruised Ego ... 151
    10. Perjury ... 181
    11. Conspiracy ... 199
    12. The Scales of Justice ... 219

Epilogue
    Character on Trial ... 235
    Notes and References ... 255

Author's Note

All conversation, which is placed in inverted commas throughout this book, is the reported conversation given by first-hand witnesses as they gave evidence on oath, or were quoted by newspaper reporters.

Prologue

Ernst Büttner on Trial

> In England for many years past, the death penalty has not been carried out for crimes in which life has not been lost.
>
> **Sydney Morning Herald, May 10, 1889**

On Tuesday morning, March 19, 1889, Ernst Büttner appeared before Stipendiary Magistrate Addison at Sydney's Water Police Court charged with the rape of eighteen year old Jessie Lennox. Aged twenty-eight and born in Germany, Büttner's name was anglicised by the courts and the newspapers, and recorded as Ernest Buttner. He was represented by barrister David Buchanan, instructed by solicitor William Patrick "Paddy" Crick.

Sergeant Murphy deposed that he had been called to Büttner's boarding house in Erskine Street at 12:45 earlier that morning, and had subsequently arrested him.

Jessie Lennox testified that she had arrived in Sydney from Brisbane on Sunday, just two days ago and, on the advice of another passenger, she had gone to Büttner's boarding house wanting to stay there until she found employment as a domestic servant. On the Sunday night, she stayed in a room on the ground floor, but the next day Büttner moved her to a room upstairs. On Monday night she retired to bed about ten o'clock, leaving a candle alight. Half an hour later, the accused entered her room with two bottles of drink. When

Prologue

she declined to have a drink, he threatened to ram the bottle down her throat. He then raped her. She managed to jump out the window, landing on the roof of an outhouse, a drop of about two metres. She screamed until rescued by a policeman and two gentlemen. Evidence was also given by three men from the boarding house of finding her in distress.[1]

Magistrate Addison adjourned the court to the following day so as to receive evidence from the Police Surgeon, Dr William Strong. The doctor deposed that he had examined Jessie Lennox when she was brought to him in the early hours of Monday morning. He found that she had been assaulted with great violence; at the time of the assault the girl had been a virgin.

Büttner reserved his defence. Magistrate Addison committed him to stand trial for the rape of Jessie Lennox.

For his part, Büttner had not denied having sex with the girl, but claimed it had been consensual (a common defence to any charge of rape). He declared that she consented to sex with him after he brought a glass of lemonade to her room at 10:30 but, two hours later, jumped out the window and began screaming when he made advances to have sex with her a second time.

Ernst Büttner appeared before Justice William Foster at Central Criminal Court on Monday, April 29.[2] Jessie Lennox testified much as she had at the committal hearing. As soon as she could get free of him, she had escaped out the window. Barrister David Buchanan could not shake her testimony in his cross-examination. Why had it taken so long (from 10:30 to 12:30) for her to start screaming? He had his hand over my mouth, she replied.

One boarder deposed that when he heard screams, he had gone to his window and saw the girl on the roof; he also saw Büttner looking out her window.

Ernst Büttner on Trial

Ernst Büttner's prison photo on entering Darlinghurst Gaol.

The compelling prosecutorial evidence came from Dr Strong. He said that after his medical examination of the victim, he formed the opinion that she had suffered great violence; he also believed that she had previously been a virgin.

If the defence wanted to put Büttner on the witness stand, they could not as this was not permitted by the justice system at this time (it was claimed that a prisoner could be convicted by his own testimony).

George Way, a waiter employed by Büttner, testified for the defence that he had seen "undue intimacy" taking place between Lennox and Büttner before the offence. The prosecution recalled Lennox and she swore that this was "utterly false".

In his summing up for the defence, Buchanan emphasised the length of time between when Büttner entered her room and when she screamed. He also pointed out that she had sworn she had locked a door which the police had found could not be locked – if her testimony was wrong on such an important point, then her whole testimony should not be believed.

The jury retired for about two hours, and returned a verdict of guilty. They recommended mercy be extended to Büttner as they regarded that Lennox had been foolish to stay in an

Prologue

establishment in which she was the only female client.

Justice Foster stated he could find no fault with the verdict of the jury, and sentenced Ernst Büttner to death.

In Darlinghurst Gaol, Büttner was placed in a death cell, wearing leg chains and under observation 24 hours a day – a condemned man was not to cheat the hangman by suicide. The German friends, who visited him, were forced to converse in English, not German, as the guard listened in on all conversation.

All death sentences needed to go before a meeting of the Colonial Government's Executive Council (Cabinet) for a final decision. And this process entailed a certain amount of buck-passing: on passing a death sentence, the judge could hold the Executive Council ultimately responsible for the defendant's death, rather than himself; the Executive Council would usually advise that they believed the law should take its course, reducing their responsibility. On May 7, the Executive Council ignored the jury's recommendation for mercy, and decided there would be no commutation of the death penalty. The Governor of Darlinghurst Gaol, John Lovett, visited Büttner, chained in his cell, and informed him he would hang in three weeks – on May 28.

Paddy Crick, aged just twenty-seven at the time of this trial, was already building a reputation for the doggedness of his defence of clients. In this case, Dr Strong's evidence had been so damning, and so little was known of the Lennox girl. Convinced of Büttner's innocence, Crick made efforts to find out more about her Brisbane background.

Crick had been elected to the New South Wales colonial government earlier in 1889 (representing the seat of West Macquarie centred on the town of Blayney). Following

Ernst Büttner on Trial

William Patrick "Paddy" Crick, aged 27 at the time of Büttner's trial, was also the Member for West Macquarie in the New South Wales colonial government.

the Executive Council's confirmation of Büttner's death sentence, Crick rose in Parliament later that day and requested an adjournment from the current business of the House to discuss the Büttner case – he was adamant that his client was innocent and that the jury of twelve had reached a wrong verdict. But, as it was nearing midnight, the House closed without proceeding into the matter.

Several letters appeared in newspapers complaining of the death penalty on Büttner, but not of the conviction itself. In the *Evening News*, the letter writer claimed that as the girl had not been rendered unconscious, and as she was strong enough to escape, then the death penalty was too severe. The writer also noted that a man named Jones had recently been found guilty of incest in Victoria, and his death sentence had been commuted.[3] A letter in the *Sydney Morning Herald* stated: "In England for many years past, the death penalty has not been carried out for crimes in which life has not been lost."[4] (And the British justice system was the foundation of the Australian justice system.)

On May 11, the *Brisbane Courier* reported:[5] "The Sydney police have since been in communication with the Commissioner of Police, Brisbane, through the Chief Secretary, with regard to

Prologue

the career of Jessie Lennox in this city, and inquiries made by Detective Grimshaw go to show that she arrived in Queensland about two years ago, and used to consort with persons of known bad character At one time she was employed at a confectioner's shop in George street. She afterwards lived with a man as his wife She was subsequently charged at the City Police Court with passing a bad £10 note on a China man in the Valley, and on medical examination she was found to be insane, and was sent to Woogaroo [Asylum], from which place she was released about the middle of March last, when she went to Sydney."

Could this Jessie Lennox and the Jessie Lennox in the Büttner case be one and the same?

Two days later, Sydney's *Australian Star* newspaper published a Brisbane police description of their Jessie Lennox:[6] "She has been a little over two years in the colony, aged about 22 years, light coloured hair, strong Scotch accent, and occasionally very abrupt and flighty in her manners. She has the reputation of being a fair singer. She dresses well, and has a good stylish figure." Following this was a description by Sydney police of their Jessie Lennox: "[She was] pleasing in manner, with a full face, florid complexion, slightly freckled, sparkling eyes, about 5 ft 2 in [157 cm], stout build, full bust, brown hair inclining to chestnut, cropped rather short, and apparently about 18 years of age."

Paddy Crick made contact with Jessie Lennox and soon established that she was indeed the Brisbane Jessie Lennox, recently released from Brisbane's Woogaroo asylum. He obtained the following letter, written by her and addressed to himself:[7]

> Sir,
> Referring to the death sentence passed upon Ernest Buttner, I beg of you to use your influence with the Government to stay the same for the following reasons: -

1. After considering the matter well over I am afraid I gave some encouragement, and my conduct may have been a little eccentric.
2. Having only been released a short time-from a lunatic asylum, I had not felt well for a few days previous, and I believe I must have had a temporary relapse of my old enemy at the time and on the night in question. Under these circumstances I urge you to use your influence with the Executive Council. Meantime, I don't wish to exonerate myself from blame.
I am, etc.,
Yours truly,
Jessie H Lennox

Crick passed this letter to the Premier, Sir Henry Parkes, chairman of the Executive Council, ex officio, and also gave copies of it to the newspapers, who printed it the next day. In parliament, Crick declared the girl had written the letter "without dictation or solicitation".[8] He believed Büttner would soon be walking the streets a free man, and pleaded that Büttner be told immediately that the death sentence would not be carried out.

In a letter to the *Herald*, David Buchanan (Büttner's barrister) wrote that if the contents of this letter were true, then it was "something calculated to make most men tremble".[9] The Executive Council should consider the "instant liberation" of Büttner.

Following its printing of the Lennox letter, the *Evening News* editorialised:[10] "No man of right feeling can view with anything but repugnance for the dastardly conduct of Buttner in taking advantage of the girl's temporary residence in his house to gratify his passions, and we trust he will receive a severe punishment; but we submit that there are circumstances surrounding the case which would fully warrant the Executive

Prologue

Council in remitting the death penalty."

The *Australian Star* ran a lengthy article on the "strange coincidences" between the two Jessie Lennoxes. It noted that the Brisbane Lennox was "well and unfavourably known", she was a "degraded woman" and she was an "associate of sailors and midshipmen".[11]

A *Star* reporter managed to gain an interview with Jessie Lennox. While she agreed with much of what had been reported about her from Brisbane, she maintained that while she had been very friendly with sailors, she had not had sexual relations with them and, further, she had been a virgin before Büttner. She then agreed with Büttner's claims on the affair:[12] "She admits that she permitted Büttner to take liberties with her in the first instance and offered no resistance … when questioned as to why she did not repulse his advances, she pleaded that any harshness on her part would not be ladylike, and only women of a certain class would use such resistance. She then proceeded to remark that when Büttner attempted to assault her 'on the second occasion', she became disgusted and jumped through the window … These admissions seem not inconsistent with the statement of Büttner that she quarrelled with him only on the second occasion that he made his advances."

Jessie Lennox went to the House of Assembly on the night of May 15 and, in company with her solicitor, made statements to Mr Melville (the chairman of committees) exonerating Büttner. The next day, Premier Parkes was informed of this and sent for Melville, obtaining confirmation from him. The Premier then ordered a special meeting of the Executive Council for the next morning.[13] Following this meeting, held eleven days before Büttner was due to be hanged, the Executive Council announced their decision to commute his death sentence. But they were at a loss of what to do with Büttner – there being a great reluctance to overturn any verdict made by a jury and there was no system of appealing a verdict. The Council set up a Commission consisting of two men, Dr Norton Manning, a Government Medical Officer for the Insane, and Mr Harold Maclean, the Comptroller of Prisons, to make an enquiry into the case and to report back to the Executive Council. In the meantime, Büttner was to remain in his Darlinghurst cell. In Parliament, Crick requested that Büttner have legal representation (himself) on the Commission, but this was refused.

Governor Lovett visited Büttner in his cell and informed him of the reprieve. No longer under a death sentence, his leg irons were removed and the twenty-four observation of him ceased.

The *Maitland Mercury* editorialised:[14] "Büttner's case will be a standing example of the danger of hanging a criminal on the [sole] testimony of his victim … Human life is as sacred as female chastity. Neither one nor the other should be imperilled either by the weakness or by the rigour of the law."

The *Bulletin* was also against the death penalty for any crime other than murder, declaring this was the case in Britain, France and Germany. In his native Germany, Büttner would have been sentenced to three years in gaol. The article also argued that the death penalty for rape was an inducement for any rapist to murder his victim. The *Bulletin* also criticised the *Evening News* for inflaming public opinion against Büttner by the false claim he had twice previously been charged with "similar crimes".[15]

The *Australian Star* editorialised that Büttner had been saved from "judicial murder".[16] If Lennox had come from somewhere outside of Australia rather than from Brisbane, nothing would have been learned of her background, and it was almost certain that Büttner would have been hanged. The *Star* continued: "It

Prologue

may be true that Buttner is a low, filthy-minded brute, but even men of this class should not be hanged unless the capital crime [of murder] is committed ... it is now proved beyond the possibility of reasonable doubt that the offence this fellow committed was not legally punishable at all. It is not an action to be morally approved of, but that is altogether beside the point. From the first, all the police seemed to care about was 'getting their prisoner convicted'." The *Star* noted: "As a matter of observance, it may be stated that men who are condemned to death, and who are also recommended to mercy by the jury, preserve, until their ultimate fate is known, a composure which borders on indifference." And Büttner had been no different. Told of his reprieve, there was: "A mere bowing of the head, in which it fell almost listlessly for a moment, and then a deep breath and an erect front and a bright light over the face, all showed that the message of life had been realised. Life! But what next? Ah, that we don't know."

How long would he now remain in gaol? Days? Months? Years?

At noon on May 28, the Executive Council held a special meeting to hear the commission's report from Dr Manning and Mr Maclean. Judge Foster submitted a supplementary report to the effect that if, during the trial, he had been aware of the evidence presented to him by the commission, he would have told the jury to give Büttner the benefit of the doubt and find him "not guilty".

The commissioners' report was never made public, but an editorial in the June edition of the *Australasian Medical Gazette*[17] quoted from it, indicating the *Medical Gazette* had access to it. Jessie Lennox told the commissioners that she never consented to the sex with Büttner, and he never asked her for sex. At the same time, she did not tell him to stop, and she remained silent during

Ernst Büttner on Trial

This satirical cartoon by the Bulletin shows the Judge dragging Büttner to the gallows with Jessie Lennox about to cut the rope, while a Commissioner stands in the background with the Commission Report in his back pocket.

the sex – legally, this was a tacit consent. She also stated: "When in the asylum I know I got the character of having been on the town, and I thought when I came to Sydney I might as well earn it, and he might as well have it [my virtue] as anyone else."

Dr Strong was present at the Executive Council meeting and stated that, having heard the facts from the commission, he was "willing to modify" the statements he made in evidence at the trial.

The *Medical Gazette* defended Strong – who had received much criticism in the newspapers – and printed the delicate details of his examination of Jessie Lennox, which he gave in court, and which were otherwise unpublished: "[I] found the genitals covered with blood, the innermost part of the top of the thighs covered with blood … Upon separating the lips I found the entrance to the vagina torn, gaping and bleeding. The hymen was completely ruptured. From the condition

Prologue

of the parts, I am of the opinion that sexual intercourse had been effected with considerable violence at a very recent date." Certainly Strong was justified in this conclusion, being aware that the girl was claiming rape. But her injuries could also have been sustained by her jumping out the window and hitting the roof of the outhouse, particularly the gutter, about two metres below. The *Medical Gazette*, however, "regretted" that Strong had claimed the hymen was "completely ruptured" as "when destroyed [during intercourse, it] leaves so little trace behind". At the same time, it seems probable that Jessie Lennox had indeed been a virgin, and Büttner had been none too gentle with her, leading to her reckless jump from the window after he made advances for a second coupling.

The key to this trial was the two hours between when Lennox had initially claimed a rape took place at 10:30, and when she jumped out the window at 12:30. At no stage did Lennox suggest that Büttner left the room. If he had raped the girl, why would he hang around for two hours afterwards unless he believed she was agreeable to the sex? And there were no screams during this period. So what did they do during this time? Lay side by side? Doze off? Even when she jumped out the window and screamed – was it from injuries sustained in the fall? from her predicament? or both? – Büttner did not flee the scene as could be expected of a man with a guilty conscience.

Leaving the Council meeting, Sir Henry Parkes, entered Parliament and made the announcement that Büttner would be released from gaol. The decision was relayed to the Governor of Darlinghurst Gaol. At 4:30 pm, Governor Lovett went to Büttner's cell:[18] "Büttner, you are a free man; we don't want you here any more." Fifteen minutes later, Ernst Büttner passed through the gates of Darlinghurst a free man.

Ernst Büttner on Trial

May 28, 1889, would prove to be the most extraordinary day in the life of Ernst Büttner: not only was this the day of his release, it was the day on which he had been scheduled to hang and, even more bizarrely, it was also his 29th birthday.

Born in Saxony, Germany, Ernst Büttner had lived in Sydney for about six years. He had brought some money with him on arrival and was eventually able to buy the boarding house in Erskine Street for £400. At one stage he had applied for Australian citizenship, but had not been living in the colony long enough to qualify. While in gaol under sentence of death, Büttner was forced to wind up his affairs and settle outstanding debts, necessitating the quick sale of the boarding house, which raised a mere £150. With all debts settled, Büttner left gaol penniless – Paddy Crick not only waived his own legal fees, but paid Buchanan's barrister fees and provided him with some financial assistance.[19]

As for the Government, they just wanted it all to go away. They had no liking of Büttner; he may have been innocent of the crime of rape, but they still regarded him as lecher who had preyed on a young woman. And he was a foreigner, a German (in its reporting of the trial, the *Newcastle Morning Herald* had used the headline: "A German Ruffian Outraging an Englishwoman").[20]

Paddy Crick insisted that Büttner should be paid compensation – after all he had spent 72 days in gaol, 18 of which were in the death cell. On June 7, Paddy Crick and Ernst Büttner met with Sir Henry Parkes to discuss compensation. Parkes offered him £50 to go to Germany or San Francisco (there was a newspaper report that Büttner's mother currently lived there) or anywhere, as long as he left the country. Büttner replied that he would like to stay in Sydney and try to re-establish himself.

Prologue

Sir Henry abruptly terminated the meeting, withdrawing any offer of compensation. Crick pursued the matter, writing to the Premier and demanding compensation for Büttner. On June 17, Parkes announced the Government would pay £50 to Büttner unconditionally. It may have been a paltry sum considering, but Crick could see that a higher amount was highly unlikely – Büttner collected the money the same day.

Crick also demanded a pardon for Büttner, and he received a "royal pardon", claimed to be the colony's first such pardon signed by the Queen's representative, the Governor of New South Wales, Lord Carrington, on July 6. It began: "Victoria by the Grace of God …"[21]

Ernst Büttner was not able to re-establish himself in Sydney. In July he appeared in court charged with being drunk in Bathurst Street, Sydney, and fined £2.[22] From here Büttner disappears from the pages of Australian history; perhaps he did decide to return to Germany after all.

In 1891, Paddy Crick supported a bill before parliament that would permit defendants in trials to give evidence from the witness box; it became law. If Büttner had been able to give his side of the story at his trial, could a "not guilty" verdict have been obtained? At least, after the passing of this law, there was an added option in a defence strategy, and the possibility was there.

For Paddy Crick, this was the case that made his reputation, turning his legal firm – dealing mainly in criminal law – into one of the biggest and most profitable in Sydney.

Any wonder then, that when George Dean was charged with the attempted murder of his wife Mary – a crime carrying the death penalty – his friends went to Paddy Crick's law firm seeking his services.

Part 1
A Marriage on Trial

Love and scandal are the best sweeteners of tea
Henry Fielding
Love in Several Masques, 1728

1.

The First Wedding Anniversary

I remain your loving and affectionate husband.
George Dean

On Saturday night, April 18, 1891, at about 10:45, the steam ferry *Possum* cast off from the wharf at Circular Quay, departing for Mosman across Sydney Harbour. As the gap between the ferry and the wharf widened, two ladies tried to jump off the boat onto the wharf, but fell into the cold harbour water.

"It was very dark," the *Sydney Morning Herald* reported on the following Monday, "but the master of the ferry boat jumped in after them. One of the ladies clutched him round the neck, while he held the other up by the arm. In this position he reached the piles under the jetty, the steamer having drifted some distance from the jetty in the meantime. On being hauled up out of the water, one of the ladies was found to be suffering severely from the effects of the immersion, and is so still. The passengers on board speak eulogistically of the conduct of the master of the ferry boat, more particularly in view of the fact that he is in only indifferent health, a circumstance which he, however, did not permit to deter him from saving the lives of those in his care."[1]

George received a "purse of sovereigns" (£1 coins) amid much acclaim for his rescue. And this was not the first time that George Dean, the Captain of the *Possum*, had saved a passenger's life. On another occasion he had received a watch as a reward for rescuing a passenger from the harbour.

A Marriage on Trial

Circular Quay in the 1890s with the North Sydney pier in the foreground. The *Possum* steamed back and forth between Circular Quay and North Sydney

Captain Thomas Summerbell, the Manager of the North Shore Ferry Company, stated that George had joined his company in 1884 at the age of sixteen, recommended by George's step-father. George began work as a labourer in the yard, then worked as a deck-hand on the ferries. At the age of twenty-one, he obtained his Master Mariner's Certificate. He had been Master of the night ferry for several years now, starting work around eleven at night and finishing at five in the morning, mooring the ferry at Circular Quay, and then reconciling the night's takings with Captain Summerbell at 5:15, before proceeding home to North Sydney.[2]

Sometimes there would be a total of only fifteen passengers throughout the night, sometimes double this. George had been requesting day work for some time now, but Captain Summerbell said he not been able to find a suitable replacement for him on the night ferry. He had nothing but praise for the way in which George carried out his duties

The First Wedding Anniversary

The North Sydney wharf. The paddlewheel steamer *Possum* is moored to the right of the small boat. In 1903, it was converted into a cargo boat plying the Manning River.

during the eleven years of his employment.

James Elliott, a sub-editor with the *Sydney Morning Herald*, could remember George Dean when he started as a deck hand. More recently, he travelled home on the ferry late at night, and quite often was the only passenger. He would usually stand beside George at the wheel and talk to him for the fifteen minutes of his journey. He addressed him as "George" or "Skipper", and had formed nothing but the highest opinion of his character.[3]

On one particular afternoon recently, Elliott said, he had been playing cricket with his eleven year old son and Tom Thompson, when George happened along and joined in for a short period. Thompson was one of George's best friends; he worked as the engineer on the *Possum* alongside George, and lived in Miller Street, North Sydney, just two doors from him.

No one had a bad word to say about George Dean. Indeed he was very much a man of the people, so much admired. To friends, workmates and the ferry passengers who regularly came in contact with George over the years, it was impossible to believe anything bad of this man, let alone that he had murderous designs on his wife.

On Monday, March 4, 1895, Inspector Stephen Cotter, stationed at North Sydney, received a bottle containing lemon syrup from Dr Bernard Newmarch with an allegation it may contain poison causing one of his patients, Mary Dean, severe illness. A forensic examination confirmed that it did indeed contain poison, a quantity of strychnine. Inspector Cotter sent Sergeant Richard Brennan to make enquiries. In court under oath, Sergeant Brennan gave a report of his interview with those persons concerned.[4]

Brennan arrived at the Dean residence around nine o'clock on Thursday evening, March 7. Caroline Seymour let the Sergeant in, and ushered him upstairs to where her daughter lay sick in bed. Five minutes later, George Dean, Mary's husband, arrived home.

Mary asked George the whereabouts of baby Florence. "At Woollahra," George replied, indicating the Konnecke family (friends of George), who were looking after the baby while Mary was sick. "You did not tell me to bring her home."

George left the room.

Caroline Seymour reached under a chest of drawers beside the bed and withdrew a glass half-full with liquid. She gave it to the Sergeant saying this was part of a cup of tea that George had given her daughter to drink on the previous Sunday, and it could contain poison.

Brennan went to George's bedroom.

"Where do you get your water from?" the Sergeant asked, considering the possibility of accidental poisoning.

"From the Sydney water supply; from the tap," George replied.

"My reason for asking the question is in consequence of

your wife's illness. I thought if you got water from a tank that poison might get into it accidently."

"There is no poison in the house," George replied. "The first I heard of my wife's illness was on Saturday night last, and I gave her tea and toast on Sunday morning and also on Sunday evening. The case seems mysterious to me."

Sergeant Brennan left.

The next morning, Brennan took the tea handed to him by Mrs Seymour to Dr William Doherty for a forensic examination. That evening, the Sergeant returned to the Dean residence accompanied by Constable Weir. Their knocking at the front door went unanswered, but they entered the premises nonetheless, walked upstairs to George's bedroom, and woke him.

"I have two warrants for your arrest," Sergeant Brennan said, as George sat up in bed.

Sergeant Brennan formally arrested and charged George with the attempted murder of his wife Mary on two counts of poisoning. The first warrant charged that he poisoned his wife on Saturday, March 2.

"Very strong that," George said. "I suppose I shall have to come and prove my innocence."

The second warrant charged that he had poisoned his wife on Sunday, March 3.

"Pretty hard that, I can assure you," George said. "I had no knowledge poison was in the house."

Brennan issued the standard legal caution.

"You told me last night that you gave your wife tea and toast on Sunday morning last, and also on Sunday evening."

"Yes," said George.

"Were the vessels clean that you gave your wife tea and toast out of?"

A Marriage on Trial

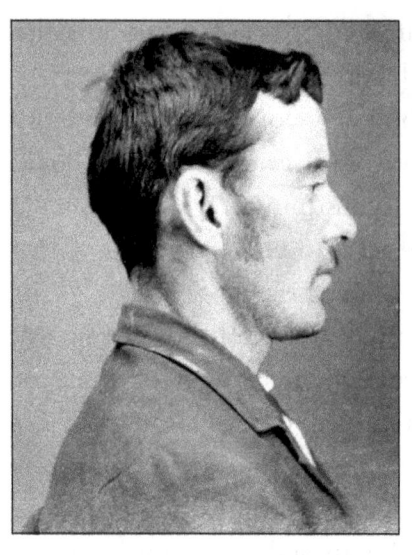

This side photo of George was taken as he entered Darlinghurst Gaol

"Yes, thoroughly clean. I scalded the teapot before I made the tea, and I got a clean cup and saucer off the dresser."

"In the tea which your wife says you gave her on Sunday morning last," Brennan said, 'arsenic has been found in it."

"Well, that's mysterious. I had no knowledge of poison being in the house. I did not wash the cup and saucer which I gave her the tea out of. The wife must have washed them up ... The first I heard of poison being in the house was Tuesday morning last. Mr Weynton, who lives next door, asked me about the poison found in the bottle [of lemon syrup], and Mrs Seymour told me the police were coming up [to arrest me]."

Sgt Brennan searched George's room, including all his clothing, looking for poison. He asked George to accompany him as he and Constable Weir searched each room in the house. No poison was found, but he took two boxes, one containing pills, and a bottle containing a "brown liquid".

"I gave my wife some lime-water and milk and a few drops of brandy on Monday night," George said, "and I gave her the medicine in the same glass shortly afterwards, and that is how the medicine had a milky appearance."

They entered Mary's bedroom, where she lay sick in bed.

"Do you want me to go?" George asked her.

The First Wedding Anniversary

"If you are innocent, you had better go and prove your innocence," she replied.

"I am innocent," he said.

Taken to North Sydney Police Court, George was remanded in custody until March 14.

In the greatest of ironies, George was charged with the attempted murder of his wife on a day most married couples would have been celebrating – March 8, 1895, was George and Mary's first wedding anniversary.[5]

On Monday, March 11, George wrote a letter to Mary from his cell in Darlinghurst Gaol, and this was duly passed on to her by the Deputy Governor of the Gaol:[6]

> My Darling Wife
> I now have liberty to write to you, hoping that you are improving in health, and baby also. I do long to know how you are getting on. Well, dear, if you go down to the lock-up, North Shore, and ask them to give you my bank-book, as there is a few pounds in it which you can draw by showing this letter.
> Well, dear, I am broken-hearted because I am away from you, but I will hope that you can be happy once more when the trial is over, as I shall prove that I am innocent of the charge that keeps me from living with you and baby.
> Well, dear, I did not think I was going to be taken away from you so soon. I thought there would be no more about it until you got well and strong. You know that they came and took me out of my bed, but, my dear, I will prove that I am not guilty of what they have taken me for.
> My dear kindly write and let me know how you are getting on, as it will be a great comfort to me to read your kind letter from your own dear self, as it will

help to cheer my poor broken heart. I cannot eat or drink or sleep for the thoughts of you; and to think I am innocent of the charge which is laid against me.
   I remain
   your loving and affectionate husband
   George Dean
   xxx xxx xxx xxx xxx xxx xxx
   All these loving kisses for you and baby

Mary took the letter and duly collected George's bank book and the £3 in wages he had just collected, being held at the North Shore lock-up following his arrest.

At North Sydney Court on Thursday, March 14, George was remanded to appear on the following Tuesday after the Police stated to Magistrate Giles that the Government Analyst could not attend, and Mary Dean, the alleged victim, was still too ill to appear.

The next day, George again wrote to Mary from his Darlinghurst cell:[7]

   My Dear Wife
   I was very sorry that you was not able to attend the Court on Thursday as I am very anxious about you and I hope that you will be well and strong and be able to come on next Tuesday as I am longing to see your dear face and baby also. I left an order at North Shore for Mr Thompson to get my money and watch and chain and books and give them to you which I do not need now as my friends have found me a lawyer to attend my case.
   I want you to send me some clean clothes up on Monday. You can give them to Mr Thompson and he will bring them up between 2 and 3 o'clock and not later and I will give him the dirty ones. Trusting you will not forget to do this for your own dear George.

A First Wedding Anniversary

Will you send me 1 shirt, 1 flannel, 1 collar, 1 tie and 1 pair of socks and 1 handkerchief.

Trusting that I will be free and happy with you and baby again as I am very unhappy at present being so far away from you. Write and let me know how you and baby are getting on. It will help to cheer me up again. I must now conclude as I as I have no more to say this time. Trusting to see you on Tuesday with God's help.

I am your affectionate and loving husband
George Dean
xxx xxx xxx xxx xxx xxx xxx
Kisses for you and baby

There is no record of Mary's personal reaction to the receipt of these letters from the man – her husband – accused of attempting to murder her.

2.

Committal

Did you drink the tea? It will do you good.
George Dean

The George Dean Committal Hearing opened on Tuesday morning, March 19, at the North Sydney Courthouse before Stipendiary Magistrate James Giles, assisted by Robert Small JP. From the outset, and over four days of evidence, the case was sensational; before each sitting large crowds competed for the few available public seats.

George's friends had begun a collection for him; they went to the law firm of Crick and Meagher, so well-known following the Ernst Büttner case. Richard "Dick" Meagher (pronounced Marr), the junior partner of the law firm, took the case.

Magistrate Giles permitted the accused to sit beside his counsel, rather than in the dock, as usually required of the accused. The *Australian Star* newspaper described the twenty-seven year old George Dean as "a little under the average height, of dark complexion, and with only the semblance of a moustache ... [he] has a careworn face, with short hair, small features, and was neatly attired in a blue serge suit."[1]

The prosecutor, Inspector Stephen Cotter, outlined the police case against George Dean. Sergeant Richard Brennan took the stand and told of his visits to the Dean residence and

A Marriage on Trial

Stipendiary Magistrate James Giles conducted the committal hearing. his conversations with both Mary and George, leading to his arrest of George.

Mary was then called to the witness box and questioned by the prosecutor. Her testimony took one and a half days. The *Australian Star* described the twenty-one year old: "She was attired in a long sealskin jacket and a soft white shirt. She wore a dark brown straw hat, and on taking her seat in the witness-box removed her dark veil."[2]

Mary deposed that she had a row with her husband on Friday, March 1. She asked him to mind the baby but he refused, saying, "I have no time, I am going out." He then complained that the baby was dirty and that the house was dirty. He muttered something about Maggie Cassin (his former girlfriend).[3]

She said to him, "Maggie Cassin is the girl you should have married."

"That is the girl I should have married," he replied, "and that is the girl I will marry as soon as I get free from you."

On Saturday morning [March 2], Mary continued in evidence, she rose from her bed and went downstairs to the kitchen. She made herself a lemon drink by pouring a small quantity of lemon syrup into a tumbler and filling it with water from the tap. After swallowing three or four mouthfuls she noticed an extremely bitter taste – the same as some tea she drank about five weeks previously.

Committal

George Dean, aged 27, and his attorney Richard "Dick" Meagher, aged 29.

She lit the fire and started preparing breakfast. Her husband arrived home and they ate breakfast together. After breakfast she began vomiting and had a "bad head".

At lunch time, she made another lemon drink and took a few sips – it was definitely bitter. She took the bottle of lemon syrup to the grocer's shop owned by the Adey family, a short distance from the Dean house. Both Ethel Adey, who worked in her parents' shop, and Bessie Walke, a customer in the shop at the time, tasted the syrup and confirmed its bitterness to her.

On the previous Monday (February 25), Mary had bought this particular bottle of syrup at Adey's shop. Ethel Adey had then accompanied Mary home, and they both drank glasses of lemon drink made from it – neither had tasted any bitterness, and neither had suffered ill effects afterwards.

Mary said she returned home, picked up the baby, and proceeded on to chemist Richard Smith, in West Street. He

A Marriage on Trial

took the cork out of the bottle of syrup, tasted the syrup on the cork, confirmed its bitterness and returned the bottle to her. Mary next took the bottle to Mrs Lydia Gail, who suggested she take it to Dr Newmarch. At the Doctor's surgery, she found Dr Newmarch to be unavailable. Mary returned to Lydia Gail, left the bottle with her, and returned home to Miller Street.

That night she went to bed between nine and ten o'clock. George brought her a drink of porter* before he left for work, and she drank it without suffering any after effects.

The next morning (Sunday), George came into her room and asked her how she felt.

"I have suffered severely from pains in the head," Mary replied.

"What would you like to drink – either some brandy or some porter?" George asked.

"Give me what you think will do me the most good."

"You had better have some porter."

George took a tumbler to the bathroom to wash it. He returned with the tumbler in the palm of his hand and his fingers around it. She raised herself in bed and saw "something white" in the bottom of the glass; it looked like powder. Turning his back to her, George poured some porter into the tumbler, then lifted it to his nose and smelt it.

"What is the matter with it?" Mary asked.

"It has turned sour."

"Put a spoonful of sugar into it – it will freshen it up," Mary said.

"No, it may make you sick," he said

He threw the contents over the balcony and went downstairs.

Later that morning, about ten o'clock, she was still in bed,

---

* Porter was a dark style of beer, like stout, popularised in the eighteenth and nineteenth centuries by London street and river porters, hence its name. Its production had ceased by the mid twentieth century

and he brought her a cup of tea. He poured some of the hot tea into the saucer and said, "Drink this."

She noticed "something white clinging to the saucer round the tea" and asked him what it was.

"It is the cream off the milk," George replied. "Drink it while it's hot."

She asked George to go and get Mrs Bessie Adey.

"Drink the tea before I go," he said.

"No," she replied.

As soon as she heard the front gate click as he left, she got out of bed and took a tumbler off the washstand and wiped it clean. She then poured two-thirds of the tea into the tumbler and hid it on the floor, out of sight, underneath a chest of drawers. She left the remaining tea in the cup (suggesting she had drunk most of the tea and left mainly tea-leaves).

George returned with Bessie Adey .

"Did you drink the tea?" he asked.

"Yes," she replied.

"It will do you good," he said, and took the cup and saucer downstairs.

She was sick, vomiting and purging (diarrhoea) on Sunday and Monday. Dr Newmarch came to the house on Monday night, and prescribed some medicine for her. At about ten o'clock, the same night, her husband came to her bedside.

"This is your medicine," he said. "Drink it."

She looked at the tumbler and saw it was milky, and the top looked like curdled milk.

"What is that?" she asked.

"It is a powder which was ordered to be put into the medicine," George replied, as he used a spoon in the medicine to crush it.

She drank the medicine and he gave her a spoonful of sugar.

This studio photo of Mary was widely used by newspapers.

After taking the medicine she became much worse vomiting and purging every ten minutes throughout the night. Her mother arrived at midnight (after George had gone to work) and stayed the night with her, leaving early in the morning (before George returned home).

Later in the morning (Tuesday, March 5), George said to her: "Mrs Weynton has spoken to me about poison being in the syrup bottle." She told him she did not know about any poison being in the bottle, and the bottle was then at Dr Newmarch's. He asked her why she had not given him the bottle to take to Dr Newmarch, and she replied that it would have been a pity to wake him.

"A pity to wake him!" Dick Meagher interjected, "You would give him a long sleep if you could."

There was no rebuke from Magistrate Giles.

Mary continued her evidence saying Dr Newmarch attended her that evening (Tuesday), and she told him about George putting powder in the medicine. The doctor went and found George and brought him into her bedroom.

"Did you put powder in your wife's medicine?" Dr Newmarch demanded.

"No, I did not," George replied.

"Did you not say the doctor had ordered a powder in the medicine?" Mary said.

"No, I did not," George replied.

Dick Meagher cross-examined Mary Dean at considerable length about her suspicions of being poisoned by her husband and who she told about them. The *Daily Telegraph* reported that Mrs Dean "was frequently cautioned by the Bench [Magistrate Giles] as to the unsatisfactory nature of her evidence". [4]

Mary stated she had told her mother about the powder in the porter, tea and medicine on Monday.

"Did you tell your mother you had preserved the tea?" Meagher asked, referring to the tea she had hidden under the chest of drawers.

"No."

"When you saw those powders, I suppose you were a bit suspicious?"

"Yes, I was."

"And I suppose you were also suspicious when you saw him holding that glass as if trying to conceal something which was in it?"

"Yes."

"You were also suspicious when you were given the tea to drink?"

"Yes."

"So suspicious that you actually resorted to a little strategy to get your husband out of the room while you could secrete the tea?"

"I don't quite understand you."

"Well, you asked him to go for a neighbour, whom you really didn't want, in order to get him out of the room while you could secrete the tea?"

"Yes."

"When your husband left the room, you got out of bed, emptied the tea into a glass, and put it under the chest of drawers?"

"Yes."

"But although you regarded the preservation of the liquid of such importance, you did not tell your mother where it was?"

"No."

"Nor did you tell Dr Newmarch?"

"No."

Further into his cross-examination, Meagher asked why there was such a long interval between when she hid the tea and when she told her mother about it.

"I did not mention the cup of tea, as I forgot," Mary replied.

"You forgot! You say you saw powder in your porter, then in your medicine and then in your tea. Then, suspecting that you were being poisoned, you carefully preserved some of the tea, stowed it away under the chest of drawers, and forgot all about it? Is that so?"

"Yes."

"When you saw these powders in so many things, had you any idea that your husband was trying to poison you?"

"No."

But under Meagher's sustained questioning, Mary admitted that she did believe she was being poisoned.

Magistrate Giles cautioned Mary to be careful about giving contradictory evidence.

"That being so," Meagher continued, "I would ask you how was it, when your husband was giving you a glass of stout [porter] in which you could see some powder, that you asked him to put some sugar in the drink to freshen it up?"

Mary hesitated before answering: "I do not know that I had

any reason for asking the sugar to be put in."

Dr Bernard Newmarch deposed he had first attended Mary Dean when she gave birth on December 26 last year, and she had been under his care since then. George Dean had called at his surgery at about 6:30 p.m. on Monday March 4, and asked him to attend his wife. He arrived at the Dean house around 8:10 and examined Mrs Dean: she was pale; her skin moist; her tongue clean; her stomach region was tender; and her pulse regular with good volume. He gave her a prescription and strict instructions as to her diet.

The next day, the husband came to the surgery and asked him to again visit his wife. Returning to the Miller Street residence, he found Mary Dean's vomiting had been incessant, although she was in no worse condition. He had reproached her for not carrying out his dietary instructions. He visited her again on Wednesday morning and also that evening, again at her husband's request. She was much better in the evening.

On Wednesday, he spoke to George Dean about poison being in a bottle of lemon syrup. Dean asked him to take any steps to find out about it, and how it was administered. Mrs Seymour was there when he visited Mrs Dean on Thursday, and she told him about a powder in the medicine. He went downstairs, woke Dean up, and brought him to his wife's bedroom.

"Did you put a powder in the medicine on Monday when you gave it to your wife?" he asked him.[5]

"You know I did not," Dean said to him.

On December 30, the Sunday after Mrs Dean's confinement, he had attended both Mrs Dean and Mrs Seymour for an attack of vomiting and purging. On January 14, Mr Dean came to his surgery and asked for a prescription for his wife as she had suffered another attack of vomiting and purging. He wrote out the prescription but did not visit Mrs Dean.

"On each occasion when Dean came to you," Meagher asked Newmarch in cross-examination, "did he appear anxious and distressed about his wife's illness?"

"Yes."

Meagher questioned the Doctor about poisons. Newmarch stated that strychnine had a bitter taste while arsenic was tasteless. Mrs Dean's symptoms are compatible with arsenical poisoning. If you put arsenic in tea, it would run in little white lumps.

At the conclusion of Dr Newmarch's evidence, as his deposition was being checked by the Bench, some remark caused Mary Dean to smile. Dick Meagher loudly drew the court's attention to it. The *Australian Star* noted that Magistrate Giles admonished her "with a good deal more harshness than was justified" saying to her: "I must say, madam, that your levity is highly improper and indecent, and considering the serious position in which your husband stands, such conduct is scandalous."[6]

William Hamlet, the Government Analyst, deposed that he had received the bottle of lemon syrup and analysed its contents. The bottle contained 2¾ fluid ounces of lemonade, its capacity being 24 fluid ounces. There was a dense white substance at the bottom of the bottle. His analysis found 1.75 grains of arsenic, together with 1.54 grains of strychnine, the latter giving it an intense bitter taste. He had analysed the 2½ fluid ounces contents of a medicine bottle; it contained 3 grains of white arsenic, together with distinct traces of strychnine. The sample of Mary Dean's urine, which she had passed on March 9 and 10, contained arsenic. He examined her nightdress stained with faecal matter caused by her diarrhoea; he found it to contain distinct traces of arsenic. He had also

Committal

examined a small phial labelled "milk drawn from the breast of Mrs Dean", but it did not contain poison. Other samples he had been given did not contain poison.

In cross-examination, Meagher asked Hamlet the amount of poison required for a fatal dose: from three-quarters of a grain to three grains. Did Hamlet know George Dean? Yes, Hamlet replied, living on the North Shore, I have often travelled on the ferry and have become acquainted with him. What sort of a man was he? The accused seemed to be an upright man; I was present when the accused was presented with a watch for saving a life at Mosman.[7]

William Doherty, Hamlet's laboratory assistant, testified that he had examined the tumbler of tea and milk containing 6 fluid ounces. He found traces of arsenic amounting 0.1 grains; he did not test for strychnine. In cross-examination, he stated that 2.5 grains of arsenic would constitute a fatal dose. In his opinion, if the small amount of 0.1 grain was put into the tea, it would not produce lumps round the top.

Following the analytical evidence of her urine and nightdress, there could be no doubt that Mary Dean had been poisoned. The poison in the lemon syrup and medicine had not proven to be fatal doses, but they had made her violently sick. The poison in the tea was a minute amount.

The prosecution called North Sydney chemists who had dispensed prescriptions for the Deans. In cross-examination, William Guise stated that the prisoner had been in an excited state when he came for a prescription on March 2; he wanted it made up in a hurry, and went off in a hurry. Did he ever sell poison to the defendant? No. Chemists Arthur Street and Thomas MacDonald also stated in cross-examination that they had never sold poison to the defendant. The fourth chemist,

Richard Smith, stated that Mrs Dean had brought a bottle of lemon syrup to him on March 2; he tasted it and found it bitter sweet. Meagher did not cross-examine.

Even as the committal hearing was proceeding, police were continuing to check chemists' (legally required) poison books recording all their sales of poison – and giving Dean's description – in an ever widening circle from North Sydney.

Ethel Adey confirmed that she had accompanied Mary home from her parents' shop with the bottle of lemon syrup on February 25; she drank from it and it tasted sweet. Bessie Walker stated that she was in the Adey shop when Mary returned there with the lemon syrup. She tasted it; it was bitter; and she was sick afterwards.

William Gail deposed he was a furniture broker living about a mile and a half [2.4 km] from the Deans. He had received the bottle of lemon syrup from Mrs Dean on Saturday, March 2. He had drunk some from a cup after adding water but found it too bitter to drink. He had spoken to George Dean that evening, but did not told him about the lemon syrup. Dean said his wife ill. He took the bottle to Mr Guise, the chemist, but he said he was too busy to analyse the syrup. Mrs Seymour tasted it on Monday and also found it bitter. He took it to Dr Newmarch Monday evening. Dean had said to him on one occasion that he and his wife would be happy when Mrs Seymour moved out of their house.

Dick Meagher recalled Mary to the witness box. On the previous occasion when you were ill and Dr Newmarch prescribed your medicine, he asked, did you complain to the Doctor, or anyone else, that you had been poisoned? No

Before her marriage, she had lived with her mother. Her father was dead.

"While living in Little Norton Street, Surry Hills, before your marriage, were there any other inmates in the house?" Meagher asked.

"Yes," Mary replied.

"One named Jones?"

"Yes."

"I suppose this is the first intimation you have had that Jones is a criminal?"

"It is."

"Do you remember the Melbourne boys coming over to see Jones – a one-eyed fellow named Jack, for instance?"

"Yes."

"Is this the first time you have heard that this gentleman was a housebreaker?"

"Yes."

"The one-eyed man wasn't the only visitor was he?"

"No, there were others."

"You also lived in Riley Street, did you not?"

"Yes."

"Did you know a family there named Rose?"

"Yes."

"Did any of the inmates – girls predominating I believe – ever come over to see your mother?"

"Yes."

"Take plenty of time to reflect. I don't wish to lead you into a cul-de-sac."

Mary admitted that she had spoken to Mrs Rose, who lived diagonally across the road from her mother's fruit shop. She had never seen her mother go into Mrs Rose's place. Yes, she had heard that she was called Madame Rose. Yes, she had heard the place was a notorious brothel.[8]

As Mary was gave evidence, the *Australian Star* noted, George took "copious notes".⁹

The prosecution called Mrs Caroline Seymour. She deposed that she was a widow and currently living with her daughter Mary (evidently having moved into the Miller Street residence following George's incarceration). When her daughter was confined, George sent for her – she produced his telegram as evidence – and she went to their house and nursed her daughter. She was there a month before she gave birth on December 26, and a month afterwards. After that she went and boarded with Mrs Johnson at Surry Hills for a month, and subsequently became a live-in servant with Mrs Lees at McMahons Point, two to three miles from the Deans.

On Monday evening, March 4, she went to Mr Gail's house. She tasted the lemon syrup and it was very bitter. She then went to her daughter's place. On the way she walked passed George, but they didn't speak. Her daughter was very ill. She was present the next day when George denied to Dr Newmarch that he put a powder in his wife's medicine, contradicting his wife.

During Mary's confinement, both she and Mary had been sick after eating some food.

"Who prepared the food?" Inspector Cotter asked.

"I did," Caroline replied. "I left it on the dining room table to cool."

"Was Mr Dean present?"

"He entered while it was on the table."

"Did you make beef tea for Mrs Dean?"

"Yes, several days afterwards."

"Who was in the house?"

"The accused and my daughter."

"Was he present when you gave it to her?"

"Yes, he was sitting at the foot of the bed."
"Did Mrs Dean drink it?"
"She tasted it and said it was very bitter, so I threw it away."
"Were you friendly with Mr Dean?"
"Yes."

As Dick Meagher rose to cross-examine her, Caroline Seymour obviously feared a hostile questioning and complained to Magistrate Giles that it was very hard for her to be there alone, without a solicitor. The Magistrate reassured her that Inspector Cotter was representing the Crown (meaning he could lodge objections to Meagher's questions), and all she had do was tell the truth. You do not have to be nervous, Meagher said to her smoothly, the truth will prevail.

"When you and your daughter were ill," Meagher asked, "did you say to her there must have been poison in what you had eaten?"
"No."
"Failing to discover anything wrong with the food, did you form any conclusions?"
"No, I did not know what was wrong."
"Is George the class of man to poison his wife?"
"No, but I did not like the way he treated his wife."
"Did you hear that Dean asked his wife to have a doctor twice, and on the third occasion insisted?"
"I did not. He was very distant towards her."
"However, if you heard that Dean begged his wife to have a doctor, would you class that an unkind or distant action – would it not rather indicate love?"
"I should think so."
"Did your son-in-law order you to leave the house at Mosman?"
"No. He told Mrs Dean [to tell me] that I would have to go.

He told me to leave the house at North Sydney several weeks after the birth of the child."

"Did your daughter faint while the scene was going on?"

"Yes. Her husband pushed her away, and she fell into my arms and sobbed and cried."

"If anyone has said that you were speaking angrily when Mrs Dean revived, it is incorrect?"

"Yes."

Meagher moved on to Caroline's past history. When she lived in Norton Street Surry Hills, she took in boarders. One of the boarders was Thomas Jones. She had never seen him act as a fence, selling stolen property, but she had known him to have a job which earned him £7 per week. She had never gone under the name of Mrs Jones, and had never resided with him as man and wife. He had left her house about eighteen months ago. Yes, Melbourne men came to her house. They started coming about three years ago. She believed they were bookmakers. The man with one eye was named Simon; she had not seen him for some time. No, she did not know that he was serving time for burglary.

Meagher turned to Madame Rose and the brothel.

"Did you ever take charge of her house?"

"I slept there three or four times when Madame Rose was away."

"What did you do there?"

Brothel owner Madame Rose

Committal

"I went to mind the bedroom of Madam Rose."

"What went on while you were in the house?"

"I cannot say. I only had charge of the bedroom."

"Did you on any occasion go to a certain house and ask a young woman to go to the house?"

"I took several notes from Madame Rose to girls."

"Was it less than a dozen?"

"I cannot tell."

"Were you paid to take the messages?" Magistrate Giles asked.

"Yes."

"Did you know what the girls went to the house for?"

"No."

This completed the defence.

Magistrate Giles formerly committed George Dean to stand trial on the first charge (that on March 2 he administered poison to his wife in lemon syrup) but dismissed the second charge (that on March 3 he gave her poison in her tea) on the ground that the prosecution had not produced the evidence for it. Meagher requested bail, claiming the evidence presented by the prosecution was extraordinarily weak. As much as he would like to grant bail, Magistrate Giles replied (making clear his obvious thoughts on the case), no magistrate could grant bail on such a serious charge. George was returned to his Darlinghurst holding cell.

The prosecution believed it had an open and shut case. The forensic evidence proved that Mary had been poisoned; there were only two people living in the house at the time; and George admitted preparing and administering food, drink and medicine for her.

The Attorney-General's department scheduled the trial for

less than a fortnight later, and the Attorney-General decided to lead the prosecution himself.

For the defence, their client was a well-known, respected character, for whom it was inconceivable that he would poison his wife – even his mother-in-law, so at odds with him, had conceded this in her testimony. On the other hand, his wife and mother-in-law were connected with criminals and prostitutes; could their evidence be trusted?

The case was highly circumstantial. George was the obvious suspect as the poisoner but was it *beyond a reasonable doubt?* No poison had been found in the house, and there was no evidence of Dean either obtaining or ever being in possession of poison. What was his motive? Squabbles with his wife? And it was against his apparent character. Yet the defence's major problem remained: If George was innocent, how did the poison get into the lemon syrup and medicine? If not George, then who poisoned Mary?

3.

The Hanging Judge

We thank Your Honour for the clear way you have put it.
Foreman of the jury

On Thursday morning, April 4, George Dean appeared before Justice Sir William Windeyer at Sydney's Central Criminal Court. Barrister John Want, the Attorney-General, led the prosecution assisted by barrister Charles Wade. This was the first time in fifteen years that an Attorney-General had conducted the prosecution of such a criminal case – he evidently believed the case, highly publicised, to be straight forward and of some political benefit to him. Remarkably, solicitor Richard Meagher conducted the defence without employing a barrister as normally expected in such a high profile case. Indeed there was some disdain directed at the youthful Meagher from the prosecution and the judge for his wearing of mufti during the court's proceedings – no legal wig or gown and his suit was regarded as "sartorially gay".[1]

William Charles Windeyer, an only child, arrived in Sydney as a baby with his parents in 1835; his father subsequently died when he was thirteen. Educated at the Kings School, Parramatta, and Sydney University, Windeyer was admitted to the bar in 1857, aged twenty-three. He formed a long association with Henry Parkes, first as a law reporter for Parkes' Empire newspaper and, secondly as a politician. In 1876, Windeyer was appointed Attorney-General in the Parkes Ministry. On the day after his resignation from parliament in

1879, he was appointed a judge on the Supreme Court. Many of his judgements on the Supreme Court were highly praised, and he was knighted in 1891.

But his behaviour as a judge in criminal cases was highly controversial. In his book, *History of Criminal Law in New South Wales*, 2002, Dr Gregory Woods wrote:[2] "Windeyer, the judge, was a forceful man, if not a judicial bully, who brooked little dissent in his courtroom; but, as he showed in the Mount Rennie case, he had a crusading impulse (instilled by his mother Maria and by his wife Mary …) to protect the female victims of social oppression and inequality."

Windeyer had a great faith in his ability to tell whether a witness was lying or telling the truth. He castigated juries who returned a verdict of innocent against his own conclusion. In Wagga Wagga in 1888, he congratulated a jury for reaching a "guilty" verdict as "the only conclusion that rational men could arrive at", and that the "not guilty" verdict brought in by a jury in his courtroom on the previous day at Deniliquin had been "a disgrace".[3]

Windeyer reached the heights of controversy as the presiding judge in the Mount Rennie case in 1886. A girl was gang raped by up to twenty young men at Mount Rennie (in Moore Park, Sydney). Eleven men, most in their late teens, were placed on trial for this horrendous crime, and nine were found guilty and sentenced to be hung by Windeyer – four were eventually hanged.

The Mount Rennie controversy revolved on two main aspects.

Firstly, the girl was unable to identify any of the rapists. The rapes were watched by a large number of young men and the main defence of those arrested and charged was their admittance of a presence at Mount Rennie but not of being a rapist

The Hanging Judge

(Windeyer declared those watching were as guilty as the rapists and ought to be hung also). Those on trial were mainly identified by two men who wished to avoid being charged themselves.

Secondly, the conduct of Judge Windeyer during the trial was highly criticised. His summing up at the trial was regarded as biased and fully supportive of the prosecution. He forced marathon sittings of the court. The first two days of this six-day trial were of 11 hour's duration; the third and fourth 9½ hours (he attended public dinners on these nights). The fifth day lasted 18½ hours from 9:00 am Friday morning until 3:30 am Saturday morning; court resumed just 5½ hours later at 9:00 am. The sixth day went from 9:00 am until 11:00 pm, the court then having sat for 48½ hours with a mere 5½ hour break. Lawyers and prisoners slept fitfully at stages not concerning them; jurors nodded off at various times. As midnight approached Judge Windeyer warned that if proceedings were not concluded by that time, the jury would be locked up during the Sabbath, and would not return until Monday morning. The prosecution had already presented their case, and one defence counsel, Barrister Thomas O'Mara, subsequently complained in a letter to Governor Carrington that he consequently had the choice to either greatly condense his defence speech to the jury or risk offending them – he chose the former – and his client was on trial for his life.[4]

The situation was further exacerbated when the hangman botched the hanging; three of the four slowly strangled to death instead of an instantaneous snapping of the neck and death. Juries became more reluctant to convict in hanging-offence cases. The *Bulletin* newspaper, Judge Windeyer's most trenchant critic, gave him the sobriquet of "The Hanging Judge". Ironically, back in 1861, a youthful and idealistic

47

Windeyer had spoken against the death penalty believing that "society had no right to sit in judgement which would entail the death of a fellow creature".[5]

So here was another trial for Judge Windeyer in which the alleged victim was female. Surely Dick Meagher would have preferred any other judge to be presiding on the Bench.

Following the empanelling of twelve men on the jury, Judge Windeyer asked the Attorney-General Want how long he expected the case to last, if more than a day then arrangements would be needed to be made for the jury. Want replied that it would take at least a day. Windeyer prepared the jury for a marathon sitting. The *Australian Star* reported:[6] "His Honour then remarked that there appeared to be some misapprehension about the retirement of juries. When a jury retired it did so to consider its verdict, and not to go to bed. It was well that juries should know this." The trial lasted three days.

In his opening address for the prosecution, Attorney-General Want outlined the evidence against the accused. He told the jury that after he presented his evidence they could only come to one of two conclusions: that the accused administered the poison with the intent of causing the death of his wife, or that his wife and his mother-in-law had entered into a conspiracy to get Dean out of the way by bringing this charge against him. The defence had proffered this second conclusion at the committal hearing and he had no doubt they would use it again. While Mrs Seymour and her daughter did not bear the best of characters morally, the defendant had been well aware of this when he married his wife, for better or for worse. While the defendant had previously borne an extraordinary good character, and had received medals for his bravery, sometimes such persons were induced to commit great crimes.

Mary Dean, the first prosecution witness, gave evidence for five hours – the *Sydney Morning Herald* described her as "calm and collected".[7] Her evidence under Want's questioning was much as she stated at the committal hearing.

She and her husband had begun to live on unfriendly terms about a month after their marriage, and then it got worse. About three weeks before the birth of the baby she asked him to be kind to her. He said, "No." He would see her through her trouble and then leave her. There was no definite cause of their quarrel, but it arose out of his sulkiness. He never spoke to her for a week before the baby was born. After she was born, he told her he was not the father of the baby and that she was keeping another using his money. Neither was true.

Meagher began his cross-examination by probing when she became suspicious of being poisoned. It was when she saw powder in the porter. Yes, she did say to her husband, "Oh, put some sugar into it and liven it up a bit", but if he had done so, and offered it to her, she would have refused it and accused him of putting something in it. Yes, her husband had insisted on fetching the doctor to attend her; on Monday between five and six o'clock, he had said to her: "I will stand this no longer, you will and must have a doctor." When the doctor came, she did not tell him of her suspicion of being poisoned nor did she tell him about the tea she had hidden under her bed. Her mother came about midnight on Wednesday, after George had gone to work; her mother asked what had made her ill, but she did not tell her that she thought she was being poisoned by George; nor did she tell her about the tea as she was very ill and had forgotten about it.[8]

Meagher questioned Mary on her husband's character. George

A Marriage on Trial

The opposing counsel were Charles Pilcher QC, left, for the defence, and John Want QC for the prosecution. Both were Members of the Legislative Council.

had never been violent to her, she said, but he had often spoken cruelly to her. He earned £3 per week and, for the first four months, gave her £2 per week for the house, but she had not been getting it regularly since. He owned a block of land before they were married, and bought a second block after their marriage, then fenced it. He intended building a house. She had only seen him under the influence of drink on two or three occasions.

Did she have a life insurance policy which would benefit her husband on her death? No. She had an insurance policy when they married but he asked her to discontinue it.

Meagher probed her family background. Mr Jones was boarder at her mother's house; he was a tailor; she had known him ever since she was a little child. Some gentlemen came and visited him and stayed there; they were bookmakers. She did not know that Jones was receiver of stolen goods. She knew that Madame Rose's house across the road was a brothel. No, she never went there. No, she did not play the piano there. No, she did not carry notes from there. No, she had no memory of women from Rose's place staying at her house while police raided Rose's house. Yes, her mother did take charge of that establishment while Madame Rose was away, but she was only staying there to look after Rose's silver and jewellery. She did not think George had seen her mother going there. She had never told George about Madam Rose's place.

Prosecutor Want re-examined Mary on Meagher's insinuations against her and her mother. There was no truth in the suggestion she had a child before her marriage; she had led a "pure life"[9] before her marriage. There was nothing about her mother's house in Surry Hills that would lead George to think there was anything wrong about her. The relationship of her mother with the house opposite them (recently revealed) may have come as a surprise to George.

In his opening address to the jury, Prosecutor Want stated that enough poison had been administered to Mary Dean to kill several persons but she had survived because she had been given both arsenic and strychnine, and strychnine was an antidote to arsenic.[10]

The statement, that the two poisons were antidotes, was utterly false but a common belief held at the time, caused by the opposing effects of the two poisons on the heart – their combination did not affect the lethality of the poisons.

Dr Bernard Newmarch gave a much more detailed account of the forensics of the case than at the committal hearing. In his Judge's Notes, Windeyer recorded the doctor as stating: "Arsenic will continue in the system for some time, that is why I got her urine. It will disappear in three or four days after an ordinary medical dose. Finding it at the end of six days would indicate a large dose. The symptoms described would arise from large doses, not small constant doses. I also prescribed the tonic on the last day I attended her. It is quinine and iron, and a very small quantity of strychnine, not enough to do any harm. There are less than two drops of liquor strychnia in each dose, half dram [0.89 grams] in 8 ounces [186.80 grams]. It is the ordinary medical prescription ... Supposing a person took a dose of arsenic and then took strychnine, it would be an antidote to it. Arsenic deadens the pulse, but strychnine would quicken it."[11]

In a newspaper interview given after the trial, Newmarch said: "I stated that strychnine might act as an antidote, if retained in small quantities, and obviate these symptoms of collapse, by serving to keep up the heart's action and give a pulse such as found in this instance."[12] In the same interview he stated that he had thought at first that Mary's illness was due to ptomaine poisoning, possibly suffered after eating tinned food – and this was because she had a normal pulse (rather than the slower pulse expected in arsenical poisoning).

Newmarch also stated that he had been experimenting, specifically for this case, by ingesting very small amounts of arsenic to see how long it would remain in his urine. Arsenic was tasteless while strychnine had a bitter taste. In cross-examination he stated that a man may die taking half what he took; many would be able to take half a grain with safety (his doses were less than this). He never thought that Mary Dean's condition was critical, that she would die.

William Hamlet, the Government Analyst, declared that 2½ grains of arsenic was a fatal dose and ½ a grain of strychnine

The Hanging Judge

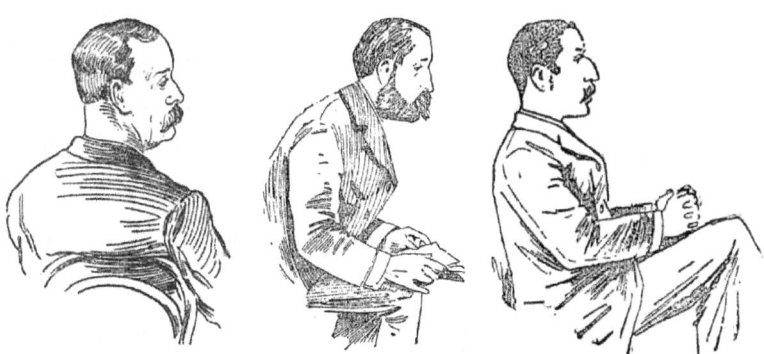

Three medical men who gave evidence were Dr Bernard Newmarch, Mary's Doctor; William Hamlet, the Government Analyst; Dr George Rennie, the Government Pathologist.

was a poisonous dose. The mixture of arsenic and strychnine would cause one to counteract the other. The lemon syrup contained 1¾ grains of arsenic and 1½ grains of strychnine. On examining the tonic, he found 3 grains of arsenic in it, and "distinct traces" of strychnine in it. He had found traces of arsenic in the faecal matter on her nightdress as well as her urine. He found just over 1 grain of strychnine in the tea, and had confirmed his assistant's finding of traces of arsenic in it.

Dr George Rennie, a Government Pathologist, had heard the evidence given by Dr Newmarch and agreed with it. Mary Dean's symptoms were those of arsenical poisoning. Finding arsenic in her urine six days after would indicate a large dose of arsenic. Strychnine, taken with arsenic, would account for her steady pulse – arsenic deadens the heart's action, strychnine stimulates it.

In this Victorian period, it was not unusual for prescriptions to contain "medical doses" (very small amounts) of strychnine or arsenic, due to their effect on the heart. Also, arsenic was taken by women cosmetically to whiten their skin and give their eyes a sparkle. Chemist Thomas MacDonald deposed that the prescribed amount of strychnine had been dispensed in the tonic for Mrs Dean, and he had not added arsenic. Chemist William Guise had correctly dispensed other prescriptions for Mrs Dean without strychnine and arsenic. Those in the chain of persons who handled the lemon syrup, the urine samples and the nightdress, in their conveyance to the authorities, were called and deposed they had passed them on without interference.

William Gail deposed that the lemon syrup had been in his possession over the weekend before he handed it to Dr Newmarch. In cross-examination, Meagher suggested it was possible for him to have added poison to the syrup. Gail denied it. Gail admitted that he was currently under arrest, charged with bigamy. Meagher accused him of previously being mixed up in a poisoning case. Gail denied it. Later in the trial, Louisa Murphy, Gail's sister, denied that her brother had ever been connected to a poisoning case. (Unstated to the court was that following Gail's first wife visiting his office, Meagher had been responsible for the arrest of Gail for bigamy on the day before this trial began – the bigamy actually was very minor in that Gail had re-married before the decree nisi of his divorce became absolute. The first wife claimed to Meagher that Gail's sister had told her that Gail had once poisoned his brother but it had not been reported to police.)

The trial went well into the night of the first day, and on the morning of the second day, Caroline Seymour entered the witness box. She had made some groats on January 13 last, and both she and her daughter were very sick after eating it, vomiting and diarrhoea. George was having breakfast when she left it on the table to cool and before going upstairs. Five days later she had prepared some beef-tea (soup) for her daughter, tasted it and left it on the stove; George was in the house at the time. When she took it upstairs to her daughter, they both found it had become bitter. Mary asked George to taste it; he put the spoon to his mouth – Caroline could not tell if he actually tasted it – and he said it was all right. She threw it out. On the Monday night (March 4), she had given her daughter lime water and soda water through the night, and medicine at 4:00 am. Her daughter told her about the tea under the chest of drawers and she retrieved it.

In cross-examination, Meagher again attacked her background in Melbourne and her connection with Madame Rose.

"Have you ever been convicted of an offence?" Meagher asked.[13]

"Am I compelled to answer that question, Your Honour?"

"Yes, I think so madam," Judge Windeyer replied.

"Yes, I was," Caroline said, later stating it was for receiving stolen goods.

"How long ago was that?" the Judge asked.

"Twenty-eight years ago."

"After completing that sentence," Meagher asked, "did you go under the name of Asbury?"

"Yes, that was my first marriage name."

"Did you know a man named Jones in Melbourne?"

"Yes, I did."

"Is there any truth in the report you and he kept an improper house?"

"Me and Jones!" she exclaimed, horrified. "Never in my life."

Caroline denied she had taken notes from Madame Rose to certain women. Her committal deposition on this point was read to her, and she then admitted that she had taken such notes.

She also denied being paid to take the notes, and reversed her testimony after the committal deposition was read to her.

Re-examined by the Attorney-General, Caroline stated that she had lived with her daughter and her husband for a month after their marriage before he ordered her out of the house. She had given them the best of her furniture. She said there was a great affection between her daughter and herself, and burst into tears.

"I only have her, and no one else," she cried. "My other daughter is dead."

With the completion of the prosecution, the defence called George Dean to the witness box – Meagher's defence strategy depended almost entirely on George's testimony. The Criminal Law Amendment Act passed through parliament in December 1891, allowing the accused the option to give evidence in their own defence.* This major decision by Meagher was a two-edged sword. Although it is now accepted that the non-appearance of the accused in the witness box during his trial cannot be interpreted as an indication of guilt, this was not the case in 1895. Justice Windeyer, hearing an appeal in the Crown versus Kops case in 1893, declared that guilt could be implied if the accused did not take the witness stand.[14] Of course, on entering the witness box, he was then open to cross-examination by the prosecution and that entailed its own dangers.

In his testimony, George declared his wife had told many lies.

He had never accused her of having a child before their marriage; it was quite the reverse. He gave her £4 each fortnight

---

* The Criminal Amendment Act of 1883 permitted defendants to make a statement in their own defence, without cross-examination, but it carried little weight as it was perceived that the guilty would lie anyway.

out of his wages, and she wanted to know what he did with the £2 he retained. He told her he had bought land and wood to fence it. She said to him, "I suppose you want some of it to keep your illegitimate children." He never told her that he should have married Miss Cassin; since his marriage, he had not communicated with Miss Cassin in any way. He was very fond of his daughter, and often nursed her.

He had arrived home from work at 9:00 am on Sunday morning (March 3), but did not wake his wife; he went downstairs, lit the fire and had a bath. On hearing the baby cry, he went upstairs to her bedroom and asked her what she would like. She asked for some porter saying the porter he had given her last night had "done her good". He took a glass from her bedside table, washed it in the bathroom, returned to the bedroom and poured some porter into it. As it did not have a head, he said, "It's flat and sour." He tasted it. She said, "Put a teaspoon of sugar in it, George, and liven it up." He did not give it to her as he thought it might make her sick. He then drank the porter himself. He did not carry the glass in the manner she had sworn he did, and demonstrated how he did carry the glass. She said there was white powder in it; there was not. She said he turned his back on her as he poured the porter from the bottle; that was not true. He then went downstairs and made some toast and a cup of tea, with milk, and brought it up to her. She said she had a headache, so he poured some tea into the saucer, and put some pillows behind her so she could sit up. She asked him to go and get Mrs Adey; he did this.

On Monday night (March 4), he went to work at 11:20 and kissed his wife affectionately before leaving. He got home at 7:30 the next morning, and Mrs Weynton told him over the fence about poison being found in the lemon syrup.

He went to his wife and said, "What is this I hear about a bottle you have been drinking out of with a white powder in the bottom?"

"Oh, the doctor has the bottle," she said. "Never mind about the bottle, give me a drink."

"Why did you not tell the doctor about that when he was here?" he asked.

"Oh never mind about that, the doctor knows all about the bottle," she said.

He summoned the doctor for her. When the doctor arrived he was lying on the bed crying – crying on account of hearing his wife had been drinking poison. The doctor said, "Oh, don't give way Dean, there is no danger. But get this prescription made up." He went and got it.

He slept in a chair till 4:00 and went to work at 11:00, leaving Mrs Seymour in the house. He returned at 8:00 the next morning (Wednesday), and asked Mrs Seymour what Mary had been having; there were soda-water bottles on the bedside table.

On Thursday night, Dr Newmarch woke him up and asked him in front of his wife and asked him, "Did you put a powder in the medicine on Monday night?"

"No," he said.

"You did, George," Mary said.

"How can you say that?" he said, and left the room.

No, he did not say to her, "You would hang a man."

No, she did not say, "Why, George, you told me the doctor ordered the powder."

George declared he had never purchased or used arsenic or strychnine. He never put powder into any of her food.

In January, he brought home some meat which Mrs Seymour made into beef-tea. He never interfered with it. He went into his wife's bedroom and saw the beef-tea on her bedside table. Mary took a spoonful and said it was bitter. Her mother tasted it and said it was all right, saying, "There is nothing wrong with that." Previous to eating the beef-tea, his wife had been eating chocolates. Mrs Seymour said that was probably why it tasted bitter to her. He then took a few mouthfuls, and found it was all right but a little salty.

As to the groats, it was a Sunday morning; he came home from work, had a bath, breakfast, a smoke and read the *Sunday Times*. He went up to his wife about 10:30. She vomited a few times and he held the basin for her as she sat on his lap. Mrs Seymour also vomited. He asked why they were sick. They did not know. They had breakfast before he came home. He asked if he should get a doctor but they said, "No."

Completing Meagher's questioning, George said: "I put it down to chaff, her talking about the illegitimate children. We were on good terms. I have done what I could to beautify the home … I have done all I could to render her happy."

Attorney-General Want asked George when he first knew of the (seedy) character of Mrs Seymour and Mary. When Mr Meagher asked the questions at the committal hearing, George replied. Mr Meagher did not tell him about it before the hearing. He could not give any reason why his wife would want to poison herself, nor did he ever think she would make up a charge against him. They had a quarrel on Friday afternoon; she wanted him to hold the baby as he was about to go out on his bicycle. She said, "You never hold the baby when I want you to." The chaff about him having illegitimate children was two or three times. Yes, he did drink the porter that was "flat and sour". This was followed by further affirmations of his evidence to Mr Meagher.

Want recalled Mary, and she denied a number of the statements made by George, including that she had ever accused him of having illegitimate children.

Margaret "Maggie" Cassin deposed that she was single. Since his marriage, George had avoided her. She had seen him twice in that time; once when he was with his wife and it was at his wife's invitation; the other time, he was on his bicycle in Oxford Street.

Thomas Summerbell was a character witness for George, who had been in his employ for ten or eleven years. He would re-employ him tomorrow if he could.

"I think everything that is good of him," Summerbell said.

The *Australian Star* reported that Dick Meagher addressed the jury in a "powerful speech" that lasted three hours. Although the Attorney-General had been fair in his opening address, Meagher declared, the evidence in the case had not supported his statements. The only motive that the prosecution could produce was that Dean lived unhappily with his wife, but there was not "a scintilla of evidence" that he had not acted in a true husband-like manner during their marriage.[15]

In closing, he reminded the jury that the accused could hang if they brought in a "guilty" verdict. His over-the-top grandiloquence, typical of the Victorian era, brought tears to the eyes of some ladies in the court gallery:[16] "There is a time that will come to all of us, when the world is sinking into coldness and darkness, when the eyes grow dim, and we can barely see the forms of loved ones bending over us to catch the last accents of our voice before it becomes hushed forever. In that awful hour of solemnity, when you will ask for mercy, it will indeed be a consolation to know that you have never refused mercy [pointing at George Dean]. That will indeed be a consolation to you on the threshold of eternity before a higher Judge … If in a few weeks' time the prisoner is brought from the cold cell to face the eastern sun, and forfeit his young life, if newsboys sell the papers that describe the ghastly scene, one of the most eager readers will be Mrs Seymour … Gentlemen I have finished. I can leave this court with a light heart, conscious that I have exerted my humble faculties to the upmost to avert a terrible catastrophe, a miscarriage of justice. After your seclusion in the jury room, I trust, gentlemen, you will be able to possess the same sincerity of conscience as myself by delivering a verdict of not guilty – a verdict based on reason, justice and mercy. That you will rescue this young man from a position of peril. That you will be able to say, this day, you have done a humane, noble and generous action. That you have done something for the preservation of life."

Attorney-General Want addressed the jury for an hour and a half. His Honour then adjourned court for the day, at ten minutes before midnight.

Resuming the next morning, Saturday, the jury requested that Mrs Dean be brought to the witness box. After questioning her on George's pouring of the medicine, they questioned George on the same point. Husband and wife gave conflicting answers.

In his notes, Judge Windeyer listed the questions he asked the jury to answer:[17]

- Was she poisoned? Mr Meagher admits that she was.
- Was it by accident or on design? Repeated illness after the groats, the syrup, the cocoa [tea] and the medicine. No poison used in the house for any innocent domestic purpose.
- If the poison was taken by design, who administered it? There were only three people in the house – the prisoner,

the mother and the daughter. The defence set up by Mr Meagher is that the poisoning is the work of a "trinity of conspirators" – Mrs Dean, her mother and Mr Gail.

- Is there evidence of such a conspiracy?
- Is the defence that the wife poisoned herself to get up a false charge against her husband a reasonable explanation of the circumstances of the case?

Windeyer's summing up lasted an hour and half. He pointed out that it was necessary for the crown to prove that a sufficient amount of poison had been administered. If, through ignorance, the accused had given insufficient poison to kill the victim, he was not to escape conviction. The kindness the accused had shown to his wife (as given by witnesses) could have been contrived to avoid suspicion. The accused had borne a good character previous to this and that should be taken into consideration, but they should remember that court records showed that persons of the highest character had fallen from virtue and committed serious crimes. In this case there was not a shadow of doubt that Mrs Dean had either taken poison herself, or had it administered to her. Mrs Dean claimed she saw her husband put poison in her medicine, and Mr Dean denied this, but it should be remembered that those accused of serious crimes can be tempted to lie in court when their life is stake. If they gave the prisoner the benefit of the doubt, it must be a reasonable doubt, and one they could not get over.[18]

The jury retired to consider its verdict at 12:25.

At 5:00 pm, the jury returned to ask Judge Windeyer if the majority were justified in trying to convince the minority to change their minds. The Judge replied that the minority were obliged to discuss all the points of the evidence with a view to coming to a unanimous decision. The jury returned to further consider their verdict.[19]

By 8:30 pm the jury had been deliberating for eight hours, and an exasperated Judge Windeyer recalled them to the courtroom. The *Daily Telegraph* reported: "[His Honour] said that as the issues were so clear in the case, and they had been so long deliberating, he thought he must have failed in some way to put the matter rightly before them. He fully sympathised with juries when they carefully deliberated upon their verdict in some cases, but here the admissions by the defence were such that it was almost a scandal upon the administration of justice that the jury could not come to a conclusion. It was admitted that the woman was poisoned, and the suggestion was that she had poisoned herself; and the issue was limited to the question. His Honour could not understand the jury's disagreement unless they believed that – he was going to say – that monstrous idea that the woman had taken poison five times over. He could understand their sympathy, and a recommendation to mercy, and a strong one, too, but could the jury, on their oaths, see their way to believe that the woman had taken two most deadly poisons five times over?"

Courts could not sit on a Sunday: "His Honour further pointed out that unless the jury agreed upon a verdict [before midnight] they would have to remain incarcerated in their room till Monday morning, as the law did not permit him to do anything else."

"I hope Your Honour does not consider we are unnecessarily delaying the matter," the Foreman said. "We are thrashing it out very carefully."[20]

"I am sure you are," His Honour said, "and I sympathise with you. But as I said before, it seems to me so simple a

A Marriage on Trial

Five members of the jury and Justice Sir William Windeyer (1834-1897). Windeyer had gained the sobriquet of the "Hanging Judge" following the 1886 Mount Rennie rape case when he sentenced nine young men to death and strongly advocated their hanging – four were eventually hung. Ironically, at the start of his legal career, he had expressed a view of being against the death penalty.

matter that I thought I must have failed to make it clear."

"We thank Your Honour for the clear way in which you have put the case," the Foreman replied. The jury retired.

Seven minutes later, the jury returned to announce their verdict.

Guilty!

They also made a strong recommendation for mercy on the grounds of Dean's youth and his acknowledged bravery.

Judge Windeyer asked George if he had anything to say.

"All I can say is that I had nothing to do with this poisoning," George replied. "It has been a mystery to me since the first day I heard of it. I admit feeding my wife, but everything I gave her was free from poison when it left my hands."

His Honour addressed the prisoner:[21] "You have been found guilty of this abominable offence upon evidence which could not fail to convince any reasonable man. It has been my lot to try a considerable number of poisoning cases, and I say without hesitation that I never tried a clearer case. It is idle for you to attempt to impose upon me by saying it a mystery to you. I am satisfied that you poisoned that woman, not once, but whenever she fell sick – as satisfied as if I had seen you put poison in her food with my own eyes. Had she died, and not been here to give her evidence, the case, to my mind, would have been just as strong. The evidence you have given, so far from in any way weakening the evidence of your wife, appears to me to corroborate it in every particular. The circumstance of you and your wife living alone led to the conclusion that either you poisoned this woman or that she poisoned herself, as was stated on your behalf – a more monstrous, absurd and incredible story to ask a jury to believe I never met with in my range of 35 years' experience. I do not hesitate to say that a disagreement of the jury in this case on a verdict of acquittal would have been a scandal on the administration of justice. The jury has recommended you to mercy – strongly to mercy – and I have no hesitation in saying that that recommendation I shall not only convey to the Executive, but I shall endorse it … I do trust that, whether you live or die, you will repent before God for this horrid offence."

Judge Windeyer then passed the mandatory death sentence.

4.

An Innocent Man

> *Dear Dad, will you come and see me, as I would very much like to see you and Mother. I have now to prepare myself to meet my Maker, and thank the Lord I can meet him an innocent being, although the jury found me guilty.*
> **George Dean (letter to Fred Konnecke Snr)**

On Tuesday evening (April 9), Paddy Crick, rose in the legislative Assembly and asked Premier George Reid if the final decision by the Executive Council (Cabinet), on whether the death sentence on George Dean would be carried out or commuted, could be delayed until after Thursday week (April 18). Crick said he was "pursuing a course of investigation that would make the public hair stand on edge".[1] The Premier replied that the request was unusual but the Council was unlikely to deal with the matter before then anyway. Crick also asked if he could receive the police reports regarding the character of the two women. That was outside his department, the Premier replied, but there should not be a problem with that.

The *Australian Star* noted that "feeling runs very high in North Sydney over the case",[2] with much disappointment George had been found guilty.

The *Evening News* stated that "the judge did himself a decided injustice" in his remarks to the jury after recalling them.[3]

The *Daily Telegraph* editorialised strongly against the verdict of the trial and was highly critical of Sir William Windeyer's handling of the trial. It noted that "public opinion,

A Marriage on Trial

This devastating satirical cartoon by the *Bulletin* portrayed Justice Windeyer occupying all positions in the courtroom – Judge, Prosecutor, Defence Attorney, all twelve of the Jury, even the Clerk of the Court.

as expressed through the usual channels, utterly fails to support either the responsible verdict of the twelve men who found him guilty, or the remark of the judge, who declared himself to be 'as satisfied that Dean committed the crime as if he had seen him do it with his own eyes'."[4]

The *Telegraph* did not intend to discuss the evidence given at the trial at present, but "a very strong impression has been produced that justice is in danger of sustaining a terrible miscarriage – one which unless remedial steps are taken, may lead to fatal results".

Further: "For eight hours they [the jury] sat deliberating without being able to arrive at any definite opinion. At the end of that time they were recalled, and it was pointed out to them that unless they made up their minds they would be locked up from Saturday to Monday. Then, after the judge had given further emphasis to certain points of the evidence, he directed that if they believed their case proved, their duty was to find the prisoner guilty, even though they strongly recommended him to mercy. In seven minutes after that, they gave a verdict that was literally taken out of the judge's mouth … The attitude of the judge towards the prosecutor and the prisoner is supposed to be one of the strictest neutrality. He is there to see that the case is presented fairly according to law, but not to try it. It is a safe rule, therefore, for a judge if he forms an opinion on the evidence, which he is not bound to do, to keep it carefully out of sight."

Interest in the case was inter-colonial. Melbourne's *The Age* newspaper commented: "The judge is grossly transgressing his duty when he employs any kind of coercion whatever to force a verdict out of a jury."[5]

The *Australian Workman* commented: "The fact that a judge was able to harass a jury into convicting the accused of attempting to murder his wife will not be taken as giving the final decision in the matter. Throughout, the public sentiment has unmistakably pointed in favour of the prisoner … and, innocent or guilty, George Dean can reasonably complain that he has not been accorded a fair trial." It also noted: "Nobody believes that young George Dean, a fine manly fellow, whose gravest fault was his simplicity, attempted to murder the lady."[6]

The tabloid *Truth* used very strong language – "headstrong judge" and "craven jury" – in a lengthy article demanding a new trial. It was particularly critical of the evidence about the two poisons – considered antidotes to each other – which was used to convict Dean. Would a poisoner, really intent on killing someone, use two poisons which were antidotes? On the other hand, two such poisons would be used if there was a conspiracy to make it appear that the person was to be murdered.[7]

The *Bulletin* editorialised vehemently, firstly, on the evidence – Dean's good character; no evidence that he bought poison or ever possessed it; no 'other woman'; no real motive to sustain a murder attempt – and, secondly, against Judge Windeyer:[8] "No Judge has a moral right to sum up strongly either for or against the prisoner; his business is to give an absolutely dispassionate summary of the evidence and nothing more. No Judge has a moral right to denounce the defence as 'monstrous'; it is for the jury alone to decide whether it is monstrous or not … No Judge has a moral right to express, by word or deed, his lofty and dignified astonishment at the jury deliberating long and earnestly where a human life is at stake, or to openly exhibit his own opinions."

The *Daily Telegraph* interviewed a member of the jury.[9] When the prosecution closed, he stated, only one member of the jury thought that Dean was guilty. Then Dean entered the witness box. At their first retirement after his testimony, only four still believed Dean to be innocent. The reason for this was Dean's admission that he gave food to his wife; previous to this they thought that someone else could have given her the poison. After they recalled both Mr Dean and Mrs Dean, and questioned them, eleven were then in favour of a guilty verdict. The twelfth man thought he was guilty but did not want to see Dean hang. After Justice Windeyer recalled them, and said they could make a recommendation to mercy, this man immediately agreed to a guilty verdict – that was why they returned only seven minutes later.

The *Australian Star* reported that "a number of the most prominent business men on the Shore" had established a committee called the Dean Defence Fund "for the purpose of defraying the expenses necessary to secure a rehearing of the remarkable charge of attempted wife poisoning preferred against George Dean". Harry Paul, George's best friend, was secretary of the committee. These men were "under the conscientious belief that George Dean was innocent of the charge alleged against him". A meeting in North Sydney's Centennial Hall was advertised for 8:00 on Thursday night.[10] While this committee was centred on the North Shore, a similar committee was formed in the city centre.

Of the Sydney newspapers, only the conservative *Sydney Morning Herald* remained silent on the issue.

The Attorney-General received a letter dated April 9 and signed by "Mrs George Dean" confessing to poisoning herself, and containing the lines:[11] "… I done it, and I pray to God to forgive me, and let him off. I don't suppose he will ever live with me again, but I will deserve all I get for trying to ruin him, for he was only cross when my mother was about …" It was quickly proved to be a forgery.

As with all prisoners under a sentence of death, George was the sole occupant of a cell on the condemned floor of the east wing of Darlinghurst Gaol, wearing ankle chains and under a strict 24-hour observation. Although visitors were permitted, conversations with them were not allowed to be private and the observing warder listened to every word. Visitors were struck by his changed appearance – in convict uniform, moustache shaved off and hair cut short – and the clanking of his ankle chains as he walked across the cell.[12] And there was a flood of visitors to the condemned man, all wanting to console him.

The *Daily Telegraph* reported on the prisoner's surprising manner in the death cell:[13] "He eats fairly well, and enjoys good rest, and during the day is fairly besieged with visitors. The gaol authorities state that Dean has had more visitors than all of the men previously put to death at Darlinghurst put together. He receives them well, chats with them, invariably declares his innocence and his willingness to meet the fate meted to him by the law ... They look upon him as a martyr about to be sacrificed. Dean's visitors represent all classes of the community. Rich and poor, gentle and untutored, alike wait their turn after being admitted at the gaol gates to catch sight of the prisoner and speak a few words to him ... Hitherto it has been the custom for very few people to see a condemned man, and those that had interviews with them were generally near relatives [only]."

In newspaper interviews, Captain Summerbell said he had visited Dean in his cell. George had pleaded his innocence in front of himself and several other visitors by taking a bible and swearing on it: "This is no place for me to lie now, Captain Summerbell – you know my position. As there is a God above me, I never handled poison in my life to my knowledge. Neither would I know it if I saw it." The Captain said he believed him; if Dean were released on the next day, he would immediately re-employ him. The paper also noted that all those working on Sydney's wharves held a similar view to the Captain.[14]

The newspapers printed letters written by George from his cell. One letter was to Fred Konnecke Snr, who he regarded as a foster father:[15]

> Dear Dad,
> It must have been a great blow to you all when you heard the verdict; but never mind, don't get broken-hearted, the truth will come out some day. Well, I must send my love to all at home, and also to Fred [Jnr] and mother, for her kindness to me while I have been in gaol in sending my food; also to Mr Vandenberg for his kind attention to me while I was at North

An Innocent Man

Shore, and to all others at home.

Dear Dad, will you come and see me, as I would very much like to see you and mother. I have now to prepare myself to meet my Maker, and thank the Lord I can meet him an innocent being, although the jury found me guilty. I am innocent of the crime which they found me guilty, and I have now to prepare for the worst, which, by the assistance of Rev Canon Rich, I will be fully prepared to meet my Maker ...

Well, dears, you can imagine my feelings when I heard the amount of lies come out of their mouths in the Court, but they will repent for it some day; and after waiting nine hours for the verdict my heart was broken completely. So good-bye for the present, hoping to see you all in heaven.

[Here followed the names of members of Mr Konnecke's family, with crosses to represent kisses]

With love to you all.

Good-bye for the present,

I have to remain, yours innocently,

George Dean, R.I.P.

"But God will redeem my soul from the power of the grave, for He shall receive me."

Another letter was to best friend Harry Paul: [16]

Dearest Harry,

Will you come and see me, as I am longing to have a talk with you, and you can see me any day. You can tell Grant (the junior warden) that I would like to see him also, and others – you know what I mean. Well, dear Harry, I have now to prepare myself to meet my Maker. But thank God that I can meet him an innocent and pure man, and I put my whole trust in the hands of the Great Architect of the Universe to bear me through. Well, dear Harry, you will not disappoint me.

I remain, yours innocently for what I am here for,

G. Dean.

A third published letter was addressed to Rev J Bennett Anderson:[17]

> Dear friend,
>
> It gives me great pleasure to write these few lines to you, trusting that it will reach you with God's speed, for the comforts which you gave to me on your visit to me on Thursday. Likewise the sermon which you left with me entitled 'Death Overcome', which gives me great spirit when I read it, which I am doing daily, as I have to prepare myself for to meet my Maker.
>
> But thanks to God I will be able to meet him a pure and innocent being; and I also hope that the Lord will forgive the ones which has brought this trouble on me, and that it may please him to forgive mine enemies, persecutors, and slanderers, and to turn their hearts which has been against me.
>
> I also hope to see you again when an opportunity affords you. Trusting with God's will and wish,
>
> I remain, yours innocently,
>
> Cap George Dean, Darlinghurst Gaol. R.I.P.

Mr Justice Windeyer submitted his official report on the Dean trial on April 11 – twenty-six pages of typewritten foolscap, detailing the evidence presented at the trial and, finally, his recommendation:[18] "I would be glad if the Executive … would spare his life. I at one time thought of only recording a sentence of death, so strongly did I feel it was not a case for execution. But on consideration I thought it would be better to leave the matter [of execution or commutation] to the Executive, feeling confident as I did that the sentence would not be carried out if I reported in the prisoner's favour … His commuted sentence should still be severe."

By "only recording a sentence of death" Windeyer meant that this would be a suspended sentence – the death sentence would be recorded but not carried out. His change of mind apparently came from a fear that a sentence less than life imprisonment may have consequently been imposed by the Executive Council.

On Wednesday morning April 17, eleven days after George's conviction, Premier George Reid announced that the Executive Council had met and decided to commute Dean's sentence of death to one of life imprisonment.

The decision was conveyed to the Governor of Darlinghurst Gaol, Peter Herbert, who, in turn, informed George. The Governor told George that the chains would now be removed from his legs and the 24-hour observation would cease. As a prisoner in a death cell, George had been permitted visitors and, most unusual for such a prisoner, there had been so many. During this time, George had been quite animated, declaring his innocence to all, and apparently in good spirits. Governor Herbert informed George that all visitations would now cease, and after nine months in solitary confinement (as mandated for all long term sentences), he would serve the rest of his life as an ordinary prisoner.

"Ten years of that would kill me," said George despondently, as the reality of his future began to fully sink in.[19]

One of the basic tenets of British justice has been that an accused man should not be forced to give verbal evidence which could result in his conviction. The *Evening News* was concerned that this basic right had been violated in the Dean trial:[20] "The foreman of the jury says that Dean virtually convicted himself by his own evidence. This new system of a prisoner, being able to give evidence on his own behalf does not always work well ... A recent decision of the High Court was to the effect that, if a prisoner does not depose on his own behalf and stand cross-examination, the judge can remark upon such abstention adversely. It is thus that a man, anxious and confused because of an awful charge hanging over him, all the more anxious and confused if he be innocent, may be forced into the box to contend with a trained lawyer ... shows how very exceptional this extraordinary trial has been, and the urgent necessity that something should be done to restore confidence in legal methods."

Until the implementation of the Criminal Appeal Act in 1912, there could be no appeal to a higher court against a jury's verdict based on incorrect factual evidence given in a trial – such as arsenic and strychnine being antidotes – appeals could only be made on technical points of law.[21] Hence, a retrial, or any review of the evidence presented at the original trial, could only take the form of a royal commission.

At the same time, there was a general reluctance by governments and lawyers to see any jury verdict overturned – it was seen as a loss of confidence in the justice system. (In modern times, the appeal system is seen as strengthening the system of justice.)

But a precedent had been set with the Ernst Büttner case, six years previously. Paddy Crick had then successfully argued in parliament for the establishment of the Büttner Royal Commission, which subsequently resulted in the freeing and pardoning of his client.

Crick determined to take the same path for George Dean.

On the afternoon following Dean's commutation announcement, Paddy Crick, the Member for West Macquarie, successfully sought an adjournment of the House for a two hour discussion of the Dean case. Crick fervently proclaimed George Dean's innocence, saying, "I am as certain of this man's innocence as Judge Windeyer seems to be of his guilt."

Crick admonished Premier Reid for not delaying the Executive Council meeting until after he had provided the House with the new evidence, which he had previously promised – the Premier had told reporters, while making the announcement, that it was a life sentence as no new evidence had been presented to the Council (the *Daily Telegraph* "understood" that the Executive Council deliberately met that morning, knowing Crick intended to present his "new evidence" to parliament in the afternoon).[22]

Crick then attacked Attorney-General Want:[23] "For the first time in fifteen years, the Attorney-General – one of the men who, if Dean was convicted, would have to sit as an Executive Councillor to decide his fate – left his office, went to the court and became the prosecutor against this man ... What sort of fair consideration can this case have received today from the Executive, when the strongest member of the Executive was also the man who asked the jury to convict him ... I say this is a travesty of justice ... There is a regular Crown Prosecutor for criminal cases now."

In his opening address to the jury, Crick continued, the Attorney-General had stated that strychnine and arsenic were antidotes, and quoted him as saying to the jury: "Fortunately with the arsenic, strychnine, an antidote, was administered; so, although sufficient quantities of poison were contained in the medicine to kill several persons, fatal results did not ensue."

"I have here the letter of Dr Kesteven, which Honourable Members have seen," Crick said. "He writes that there is no truth in such a statement, and I have myself consulted eight or nine other doctors, every one of whom absolutely laughs at such a nonsensical theory being put forward ... Medical testimony, so far as I can get it, tells me that, instead of one poison being an antidote to the other, it would rather assist the other to do its deadly work, and that it was absolutely impossible for the poisons to have been given as stated without the death of the woman having been brought about."

Concerning the poison in the medicine, Crick declared: "The Attorney-General said, 'On the 4th March the accused brought up some medicine prescribed by the doctor, and she observed him pour a white substance into the glass and break it up with a spoon.' Here was this man, who intended to poison his wife, putting the poison into the cup before her eyes, and breaking it up with a spoon. I have consulted several doctors upon the case, and they have told me that about the amount of poison, which would stand upon less than an inch of the knife, which I now hold in my hand, would have killed her right then, and yet the prisoner used such a quantity that he had to pound it up!"

He added, sarcastically: "It has been suggested to me that, desiring to attract her attention to the fact that he intended to poison her, the prisoner probably mixed in a lot of flour with the poison he gave his wife."

At the trial, the mother-in-law denied she had kept a brothel in Melbourne, Crick said. He read out the sworn deposition of one man, who had been a customer to the brothel run by her when her name was Carrie Asbury – when the blinds were blue, anyone could enter the brothel; when the blinds were red it was signal of danger. During this man's acquaintance with her, she was "known to live and consort with several convicted thieves and notorious characters, namely Johnnie

Asbury, William Gamble, Denis Gaynor, Harry Bryant, Jerry Scanlon and Thomas Jones – only Asbury was her husband".

He had sworn declarations about Mrs Dean from a number of informants. One informant said that Mrs Dean had told her that before her marriage "she had lived with a captain for some time". In another Mrs Dean told the deponent that "she wished she was dead the day she married Dean". Another one said, "Oh, if only I could do something that would get rid of him". One claimed to have seen Mary Seymour soliciting in Crown Street. Another claimed to have seen Mrs Dean "with a young man" late at night on Sunday April 7 (the day after Dean's conviction) come out of a lane off Moore Park (a red-light area).

Crick said he had evidence that Mrs Dean had visited a clairvoyant: "[Mrs Dean] asked that person if her husband would get into trouble. Mind, I do not think she thought the man would be sentenced to death. My belief is this: that she wanted to get rid of him, and under our present divorce law, if the man received a sentence of seven years for an attack on her life, she could get a divorce. That was what she was contemplating. She asked the clairvoyant if the fair man – there is always a fair man in these cases – would marry her? The clairvoyant said 'No'; whereupon Mrs. Dean said, 'You do not know anything about it, because he certainly will' ... Mrs Dean told this lady that she was disappointed in her husband, and that she hoped to get rid of him; that was a month after she married him."

Premier Reid defended the Executive Council: "The functions which separate the Executive power from the judicial power in the legislature have always been very clearly defined, and it will be an evil day for this country when they become confused ... [The case] has been tried before twelve presumably intelligent and respectable citizens of this country and they have unanimously come to a certain conclusion."

"So they did in Büttner's case," interjected one member.

Mr Black stated: "I think it is a very wise thing that we in this House cannot interfere with the decisions of courts." Yet he could not think of another case where the public were so bent against a court's decision. He had conversed with hundreds, and the bulk were convinced that the evidence proved Dean was innocent.

Mr Hogue did not want to see a Royal Commission appointed to investigate the Dean case as it would set an unfortunate precedent.

"It was done in the Büttner case," Crick interjected. "If it is proved that Dean is guilty, a great public service will have been done; if it proves he is innocent, it will equally do a great public service."

Dean was a penniless man, Crick said, and a public subscription would defray his costs in an inquiry into his case. His firm would continue to support Dean, but would not accept one penny in payment from Dean (indicating he would not benefit financially from a royal commission and indirectly encouraging people to contribute to the Dean Defence Fund).

The motion to form a royal commission was lost on a voices vote.

The next day, the *Sydney Morning Herald* published a number of signed documents, supplied to them by Attorney-General Want, declaring that Mrs Seymour and her daughter were "hardworking, honest and respectable people" – these were from people who had lived in Riley Street, Surrey Hills, and were acquainted with the mother and daughter. One of the documents was signed by Rev Joshua Hargrave, who had married George and Mary, and had known the Seymour family for ten years:[24] "… Mary Seymour grew up a girl in our Sunday school, and always bore a good character. I never heard a word against her character or that of her mother during her residence here."

Paddy Crick received a letter from the secretary of the Attorney-General's Department, requesting copies of the declarations, which Crick stated to parliament were in his possession, be given to Attorney-General Want. In a letter of refusal, Crick stated that the Attorney-General had refused to give him copies of the police reports, which had been promised by the Premier. And why did he want them? Were they to be used to decide whether or not to hold a royal commission? As the prosecutor of Dean, Crick concluded his letter, and a man fully satisfied as to Dean's guilt, Attorney-General Want was hardly the person to be deciding whether or not to hold a royal commission.[25]

The *Evening News* reported that plain-clothes police had visited "every chemist and druggist's establishment" throughout the metropolitan district, asking whether George Dean, his wife or mother-in-law had purchased poison, showing them photographs; the operation proved fruitless. On seeing Mrs Dean and her mother enter a chemist shop, one constable waited until they left and then enquired of the chemist what they purchased; he declined to tell the constable.[26]

The *Daily Telegraph* editorialised strongly in favour of a royal commission. In the case of Büttner, the *Telegraph* declared, a royal commission "at the eleventh hour" brought out the essential facts which prevented Büttner from being hanged. If a royal commission proved Dean's guilt, it would be "well and good". On the other hand, if it confirmed the public's belief in Dean's innocence, the justice system would be freed from the "deep stigma" which it currently held.²⁷

The weekly *Truth* was even more savage in its editorial, particularly with Sir William Windeyer: "Whether His Honour's failings are due to the natural obliquity of his judgment or to an honest but fanatical detestation of crime, there is no doubt in the public mind that his conduct of criminal cases is intensely characterised by what Mr Crick rightly termed 'educated brutality'."²⁸

The *Australian Star* editorialised: "There is ample cause for dissatisfaction and a serious suspicion of a miscarriage of justice … nor will dissatisfaction be ended or suspicion cease till the whole matter is subjected to an investigation very much more thorough than any it has yet undergone."²⁹

For the *Sydney Morning Herald*, while it agreed with the commutation of Dean's sentence, it firmly believed that statements made by members of the jury meant that a fair trial had been held – the twelve men on the jury were *not* influenced by the judge in reaching their decision. Clearly, the conservative *Herald* believed there should be no further proceedings in the matter, and that Dean should now serve out his life sentence.³⁰

At 8:00 pm, two days after the Premier's announcement of Dean's life sentence, 1,500 people attended a meeting in North Sydney organised by the Dean Defence Fund. The Chairman said the meeting would not discuss the conduct of the judge or the jury; they were here because they believed there had been insufficient evidence to convict George Dean at his trial. Rev Bennett Anderson said he had known Dean for four years, had visited him in gaol, and believed in his innocence. He moved the motion: "That this meeting, believing in the innocence of George Dean, considers it imperative that a royal commission be at once appointed to re-open the case." The motion passed unanimously with loud cheering. A committee, including the North Sydney Mayor and the local Member of Parliament, was also appointed to pursue the establishment of a royal commission. The meeting closed with three cheers for George Dean.

Over the next ten days, meetings were held throughout Sydney's suburbs – Newtown, Manly, Balmain, Redfern, Ashfield, Paddington, Botany, Woollahra, Leichhardt, Granville, Pyrmont, Glebe, Marrickville, Waverly, Mosman, Alexandria – usually chaired by the mayor of that suburb, and all moving motions calling for a royal commission amid declarations of George Dean's innocence. Country towns – Armidale, Hillgrove, Peak Hill, Walgett, West Wyalong, Crookwell, Yass, Newcastle, West Maitland, Smithtown, Grenfell, Albury, Broken Hill, Kempsey – also held meetings and made similar declarations.

Dick Meagher obtained special permission from Governor Herbert to visit George Dean in his solitary confinement cell. Meagher reported that Dean was confined to this small cell all the time, except for short periods when he was allowed to exercise along a passage-way. In the cell he had communication with no one; he was not even permitted to speak to the warders bringing him food. Dean appeared to be much thinner (the Governor later denied this, saying he had only lost 8 ounces – 0.2 kg), and said Dean would like more food than he was receiving. He told him of the agitation for a royal commission and this seemed to brighten his disposition. Dean took a pencil and paper from him, and said it would be a relief to able to do something to "relieve the dreadful monotony" of his cell.[31]

The climax of the campaign for the royal commission was reached with a meeting held in the Sydney Town Hall (the large, ornate and very Victorian style building, opened in 1889 and dominating the city centre) on Monday night, April 29. The *Sydney Morning Herald* declared it to be the largest meeting ever held in Sydney, estimating that between 7,000 and 8,000 had packed inside the town hall, with another 5,000 outside, unable to get in. Speeches were made from the steps to these overflow attendees by different speakers to those inside, but all delivering the same message about George Dean and passing the same resolutions as those inside.

Alderman David Davis, from the Dean City Committee, chaired the meeting inside the Town Hall, and was joined on the platform by "members of parliament, suburban mayors and aldermen, and influential citizens of all callings".[32] William Trickett, a former member of parliament, moved the motion: "That considering the nature of the published evidence at the trial of George Dean, and the verdict which is arrived at, and regarding his conviction as a possible miscarriage of justice, this meeting deems it imperative that a royal commission should be forthwith appointed to reopen the case." In moving the motion, Trickett stated that the case was one of great doubt. He asked those in the audience to raise their hand if they were satisfied that George Dean was guilty. No hand lifted. He asked for those who wanted an investigation into the case to hold up their hands. Every hand was raised. The motioned was carried unanimously to great cheering.

Trickett also declared that the royal commission should be composed of three commissioners, the "ablest barrister" and "two of the most able medical men".[33]

After numerous calls, Dick Meagher rose amid tremendous applause. His speech concentrated on the plight of George Dean in solitary confinement, and did not mention Mary Dean, her mother or Judge Windeyer. The foreman of the jury, he said, seemed to think Dean was guilty because he gave food to his wife. This brought laughter.

Daniel Green moved that a deputation be appointed to take the meeting's motion to the Premier, and called for Paddy Crick to be a member of the deputation. Crick rose and said he had not intended speaking at this meeting; he would not discuss the new evidence he had obtained in the case, nor would he give it to the Attorney-General; he would only present it to a royal commission. He then went on to be highly critical of both Attorney-General Want and Sir William Windeyer. He also suggested that they should give the government five days to appoint the royal commission before the deputation met with the Premier.

The meeting ended with three cheers for George Dean.

Two days later, on May 1, the Government caved in – Premier Reid rose in parliament and announced that a royal commission would be appointed to examine the Dean case. Cheering filled the House.

The decision was welcomed Australia wide.

On the day of the Dean Royal Commission announcement, Governor Herbert transferred George Dean from solitary confinement to a standard cell, for the duration of the Commission, but he was still not permitted to talk to anyone.

At the same time, Mary Dean was a patient in North Sydney Hospital. During the trial, Dr Rennie had pointed out to Dr Newmarch that Mary was walking with a rather peculiar gait. Following the trial, the effects of the poisoning on Mary became more severe and, on April 19, she entered hospital under the care of Dr Newmarch.

Dr Newmarch described her current condition:[34] "She is

very emaciated, and looks careworn and ill. Her hair is falling out, and she is rapidly becoming quite bald on the anterior part of her skull. There is evidence of marked peripheral neuritis, or, to put it in plainer language, inflammation of the ends of the nerves, with some paralysis of her extensor muscles, especially of the feet."

Dr Rennie visited Mary in hospital and supported Dr Newmarch's report of her condition, adding:[35] "I think it very probable that she will get worse before she gets better, although I have no fear of a fatal termination."

Who poisoned Mary Dean?

Could the Dean Royal Commission provide the answer?

5.

The Secret Wedding

> *... to love and to cherish, until death do us part*
> **George Dean and Mary Seymour**
> **March 8, 1894**

George Dean was born at Albury on November 14, 1867, and had a rather tough upbringing. In an interview with reporters at Narrandera in 1895, George's mother, Annie Deane, stated she had been born in Killarney, Ireland. The *Australian Star* wrote of Annie: "The mother is about sixty years of age and has hair as white as snow. She lives in a small dwelling on the outskirts of town, and seems to be poorly provided with necessaries … at present she had to earn a few shillings by washing."[1]

The *Daily Telegraph* noted: "The strange doings of the mother and daughter, as related by people who know them, would fill columns."[2]

Annie Byrne married Irishman George Deane, a constable, at Beechworth, Victoria, in March 1865; he was thirty-four, she was twenty-two. They had three children: Rebecca (born six months after their marriage), George in 1867, and Annie, who died a fortnight after her birth in 1869.[3]

There were reports in the 1895 press that George's father had committed suicide, but there is no confirmation of this. Annie said that after she met with an accident at Crowley Creek near Mitta Mitta, she left her husband. She had not seen her husband since then, and did not know whether he was alive or dead.

Annie said she had given birth to three more children with her second husband, two of whom were still alive; her husband's surname was Finch (given name not stated) and all the family had then taken the Finch surname.[4] Annie's relationship with Finch was de facto. The birth certificates of Jane, born in 1872, and William, born in 1874, both gave the mother's name as Deane (not Finch), and did not list the father (apparently Finch), assigning the children the surname of Deane. George told friends that William had been sent to the *Vernon*.* George thought William was currently living somewhere in a country region. Late in 1895, Rebecca, who had always lived with her mother, was remanded by a court to a mental asylum.

There had been one small blemish in George's background, one that he kept from his friends in Sydney. On November 25, 1879, a fortnight after his twelfth birthday, George Finch had been convicted at the Narrandera Court of Petty Sessions of "horse sweating" – riding a horse without the owner's permission. In the court depositions, George claimed a man in the bush said he could ride the horse, while a police constable claimed he was a dishonest boy. The Bench fined him £5, but as no money was forthcoming from his mother or step-father, George had been locked up in Wagga Wagga Gaol for three months in lieu of the fine.[5]

Two years later, George's step-father deserted his mother and left Narrandera. It seems that George was then taken in

---

* The *Vernon* was a ship anchored off Cockatoo Island in Sydney Harbour housing boys remanded there by the courts for being destitute or vagrants until the age of eighteen, at the latest. There is no record of a William Finch on the *Vernon*. There was a William Charles Dean, but he is easily discounted. It is possible William could have been arrested as a child vagrant and sent to the *Vernon* under a different surname, or else sent to a different institution.

The Secret Wedding

This studio photo of a youthful George Finch playing a flute (probably just a prop) was printed by the *Bulletin*. It is hard to know under what circumstances the photo was taken given his background of poverty (perhaps the Fimister family). It was probably supplied to the *Bulletin* by the studios which took it.

by William Fimister's family and stayed with them for several years. He may have started as an apprentice in a coach-building business. When the Fimisters moved to Nowra, George re-connected with step-father Finch, and went to live with him in Caroline Street, Redfern.* His first job in Sydney was with a blacksmith's shop in the city. It was Finch who took George to Captain Summerbell seeking his employment on the ferries. It appears George had little, if any, contact with his own family after leaving Narrandera.

On his arrival in Redfern, George became best friends with Fred Konnecke Junior, the eldest child of the large Konnecke family. The Konnecke family came to love George, and this love was reciprocated. Fred Konnecke Senior, a German immigrant, had married Elizabeth Foot in Sydney. He was a butcher and lived across the road from where George resided with Finch. "[George] was at my place all the time," said Fred

---

* The 1883 Sands Directory records William Henry Finch living in Caroline St, Redfern, and gives his occupation as carpenter. Finch's son (George's half-brother) was also named William Henry Finch.

A Marriage on Trial

Ann Hughes at the Royal Commission. She told George that as his policeman father was named Dean, and married to his mother when he was born, then his real surname was Dean, not Finch. George had then returned to his original surname (unaware that his father's name was spelled Deane).

Senior. "I cannot say a bad word about him, everything good. I looked upon him as a son."[6]

Eventually, after Finch took up with another woman, George left Finch and initially boarded near the Harbour at Miller's Point, adjacent to The Rocks. But he always kept contact with the Konnecke family.

In giving evidence to the Royal Commission, Ann Hughes said that George had boarded with her husband and herself in Belmont Street, Mosman, for thirteen months, starting around 1886 – he had previously boarded with the Lawson family in Cumberland Street. George was a fire-boy (fetching coal for the boats' steam engines) at that stage, and her husband an engineer; both were now captains with Captain Summerbell's company (the North Shore Steam Ferry Company, which became Sydney Ferries in 1899). As a fire-boy George had the nickname of Springey.

George had told Ann of Finch being the name of his stepfather, and that his father was a policeman (a respectable man).

The Secret Wedding

Ann told him it was not right that he used the name of his stepfather; he should use the name of his real father. So George changed his surname to Dean, not realising that the family name was spelled "Deane" not "Dean". After that, of the few letters that came to George while boarding with Ann, some were addressed to "George Finch", others to "George Dean".

From such a poor background though, he had persevered and made a good career for himself, earning the respect of all with whom he came in contact.

Maggie Cassin was a close friend of Ann Hughes. Ann said George and Maggie had "kept company" for about three years, but it had been over for at least three years before George married Mary. Maggie had recently become engaged to be married.

When Fred Konnecke Senior moved his butchery business from Liverpool Street, to the corner of Queen and Moncur Streets in Woollahra in 1890, he asked his wife to make room for George, inviting him to live with the family (paying board). Mr and Mrs Konnecke were addressed as "Dad" and "Mother" by George. George usually arrived home from work between 8:00 am and 9:00 am, but would not go to bed until about 2:00 pm. The Konnecke family ate about 6:00 pm, and roused George about 10:30 pm for his supper before he left for work on his bike.

George was handsome and athletic. At one stage he had been very active in a bicycle club (the new craze of the 1890s). He was very careful with the £3 per week he earned – an excellent wage for a man of his background – and had managed to buy a block of land with his savings. He was sober, rarely drinking, and certainly no one had ever seen him inebriated. He was never violent or aggressive in any way. Much of his behaviour stemmed from a desire to please people. He could talk to anyone, and people – particularly passengers

The Konnecke butcher shop at the corner of Queen and Moncur Streets, Woollahra. The man to the left, with his hand on his hip, is probably Fred Konnecke Snr.

on the ferry – enjoyed their conversations with him. He was never lazy, always busy doing something useful with his hands, whether in his own home or with the Konnecke family.

Ellen Konnecke, in her mid-twenties, told the Royal Commission that George was "a very kind, good, and trustworthy fellow", a good fellow in every sense.[7]

George tended to avoid confrontation; even when he ordered his mother-in-law out the house, he did not do it personally, but told his wife to tell her she had to go. Ellen Konnecke said George could occasionally be "surly", meaning there were times when he would take offence at something, and not speak to anyone for several days at a time, but not reveal the source of the offence. (Giving what may be called "the silent treatment" or "playing no speaks", the unspoken subtext being: "If you *really* loved me, you'd *know* what was wrong.") After George was

The Secret Wedding

convicted, Mary Dean told a reporter that George had "turned frigid"[8] on her (indicating "the silent treatment") three weeks after their marriage. At his committal hearing, she said that before the baby was born he had not spoken to her for a week.

Towards the middle of 1893, George Dean went to a picnic at Cabarita (fronting upper Sydney Harbour near present-day Concord). At one stage, he participated in a dance of Lancers★ and Mary Seymour was one of the four dancers, but not the girl he took to the picnic. On a Sunday morning several weeks later, George was riding his bike to Coogee Beach for a swim, and happened to stop at a shop in Surrey Hills for refreshments – Mary Seymour served him. They recognised each other from the picnic, talked for a time, and Mary invited him to come back and see her on his way home – and he did.[9]

So began their relationship. George became a frequent visitor to Mary (usually called May). Sometimes he would leave early for work, and call in on his way through. The Konnecke family knew that George was seeing Mary, but she was not introduced to them.

"Well, George," Caroline Seymour said to him one night, some months later. "Don't you think it's time you and Mary got married?"[10]

George replied that he was not in a position to marry her just yet. But on the following night, she repeated the question. They were married shortly after, on Thursday, March 8, 1894, at St David's Church of England, Surry Hills, by Rev Joshua Hargrave.

Mary was known to Rev Hargrave as she had attended Sunday school there (until the age of fifteen). Only one

---

★ Lancers or Quadrille of the Lancers was a military style dance in groups of four.

other person attended the wedding – Caroline Seymour. She gave permission for her nineteen year old daughter to marry George, although she recorded Mary's age as twenty. As there were no other witnesses, it was necessary for Marian Hargrave, the wife of Rev Hargrave, to sign the wedding certificate as a witness.[11] The other witness, "H Woolbridge", was probably associated with the church as well. Caroline Seymour, wrote on the wedding certificate that her maiden name was "C Adams". She falsely wrote that the bride's father was "William Seymour, Dealer", then crossed out the word "Dealer" (probably meaning specialty storekeeper), and wrote above it "Deceased". George gave his father's name as "George Dean" but left a blank space where "Deceased" could have been written (suggesting that he, like his mother, did not know whether he was alive or dead).

In all probability, the marriage was consummated at the Seymour house, before George went to work.

Two or more weeks into the marriage, George took Mary to see the Konnecke family. It was then that Mary told one of the Konnecke sisters that she and George had wed. None of the Konnecke family asked George the obvious question: why had he kept the wedding secret? Any disappointment at being left out of the loop was quickly forgiven – George was so loved by the Konnecke family.

Lilly Konnecke, married to George Konnecke (Fred's second son), gave evidence at the Royal Commission that she had met Mary at the Konnecke residence about a month after George and Mary's wedding – Mary was introduced as "Miss Seymour", and she did not realise they were actually married. She did not see if there was a ring on Mary's finger as she was wearing gloves.[12]

Why all the secrecy?

The Secret Wedding

The *Bulletin* printed this photo of a youthful Mary Seymour in a "fancy ball costume".

Had pre-marital sex been out of the question and marriage the only key to Mary's bedroom door?

Was it a sudden decision? Had Caroline talked George into the marriage – certainly she believed he was a good catch for Mary – and wanted the wedding certificate signed before he could change his mind?

Everything points towards George being somewhat ashamed of the Seymour family. How much did he know about Caroline Seymour's seedy side, her visits and work for Madame Rose, and the boarders who stayed at her house?

George and Mary never gave a reason for the secrecy.

There were three in the marriage: George, Mary and her mother. Mary had always been very close to her mother and, although many acquaintances were made through the shop, they seemed to have had very few real friends.

Following the marriage, George and Mary rented firstly in Belmont Street, Mosman. Mary's mother moved in with the newlyweds, closing the Surrey Hills store and boarding house, and giving the couple what furniture she had.

Mary was dominated by her mother. From the start of the marriage Mary was conflicted between what George wanted and what her mother wanted, and usually her mother won out. It was generally believed that while Mary quite liked George, she had been pushed into the marriage by her mother, who believed George was an excellent catch – his earnings were an excellent £3 per week; he was sober, respectable and evidently infatuated with Mary. One newspaper reported that Mary told a nurse, who was attending her in hospital, that she had once been about to marry a young man, a milkman, and a marriage date was set. The milkman told her mother he was earning £2 per week, but on checking up, her mother found out he was only earning 15 shillings (less than £1), and stopped this wedding.[13]

George could read and write with his limited education, but not strongly, his spelling was particularly poor. Mary, on the other hand, was decidedly literate. She described George to one friend as a "bad writer".[14]

At the Royal Commission, Mary denied to Charles Pilcher QC that she had once called herself Rita. Pilcher then produced a letter written to George Pegg and signed "Rita Seymour", forcing her to admit it was her handwriting. Her only explanation for the memory loss was that Pegg had called her Rita (apparently the only one who did), and she had forgotten all about it – she was seventeen at the time.[15]

Pilcher also read out letters Mary wrote to Frank Brereton in the same period, but signed "May Seymour". Mary admitted

The Secret Wedding

she had been in love with Frank, who was training to be a tailor. Mary's letter to George Pegg, dated October 1891, included the sentence: "Frank has plenty of rivals, but he has no cause to be jealous, for if he only knew how much I love him, he would not be."

Pilcher read out a poem entitled "When the Right One Comes" and signed "Arranged by Rita Seymour", the first two verses of which went:

> *I can never love, the maiden said,*
> *My heart is a glacier is cold;*
> *All men I have met are the same to me –*
> *The young, middle-aged, the old.*
>
> *I have listened unmoved while men have pleaded*
> *As if they were pleading for life,*
> *And I coldly refused the boon they craved –*
> *The right to call me wife.*

With the final verse:

> *Say not fair maid, I shall never love,*
> *For Cupid, the arrant knave,*
> *When the right one comes, his power to prove,*
> *Will find you a willing slave.*

Mary was asked the significance of the word "arranged" – had she taken the lines from some book? No, she had composed the poem herself.[16]

The subtext of this rather pointless interrogation, apropos of Mary being poisoned, seems to have been that she had been

A Marriage on Trial

Lilly Konnecke, wife of Fred Konnecke Jnr, gave evidence to the Royal Commission of staying a week with George and Mary in Miller Street, North Sydney.

involved with a number of men and was a rather fickle woman – that she had never been a "willing slave" for George.

After her marriage to George, Mary became friendly with many of George's friends. Mary told them she did like George, but gave a general impression that it was more "like" than "love".

Ann Hughes, also living in Belmont Street, said she had become friendly with Mary through George. Mary visited her on one occasion and, as she was leaving, she saw a photo of George, which George had given her husband. Looking at the photo, Mary said, "I would not have married him except for the good screw he got [money he earned]."[17]

Lilly Konnecke once stopped for a week at the Dean house (in Miller Street), about six months after their wedding. When George was at home, he was always doing something around the house. He usually went to bed at 2:00 pm. He always kissed Mary when he was leaving to go to work, but she never kissed him back. She asked Mary why. She replied that she was put upon, that she suffered it.

The Secret Wedding

"[Mary] told me she liked him at first, that she was fond of him," Lilly said. "But after, her mother used to come and interfere, and she then turned against him ... her mother used to interfere and always carry on."[18].

But Mary was bitterly upset at George evicting her mother from their home – her mother was even banned from visiting, and this necessitated arranging a meeting with her mother once a week somewhere away from her home.

From this point on the marriage never recovered, it was all downhill.

Caroline may have indulged her only surviving daughter; Mary appears to have spent most of her single life serving in the shop. Mary could not cook. Following her mother's eviction, Mary went to Ann for some cooking lessons. George complained the housework did not always get done.

George and Mary moved to the two-storey house in Miller Street, North Sydney, in August, by which time she was four months pregnant. Mary asked for separate bedrooms, ostensibly so that she would not wake him during his daytime sleeping.

When they first married, George gave Mary £2 per week for the household, and this lasted for four months. He asked her to save money so they could build a house on the land he bought. He bought the materials and built a sideboard. Mary conceded that money was very tight when George lost £62 (five months pay) after he went bail for someone and they subsequently absconded. He soon gave her nothing. Although he bought the food, she said, she had to beg for a few pence to spend on herself.[19]

George Westgarth told the Royal Commission he was a solicitor. Around January last, he had a conversation with George Dean – while travelling home on the *Possum* late at night – and George asked him whether a couple could get a divorce by mutual consent. He had replied, "No."[20] In 1895, a "guilty party" was required to obtain a divorce, and adultery was the most common ground (divorce by mutual consent did not become law in Australia until 1975).

In this Victorian age, a marriage break up was quite scandalous and, even if a couple only separated, a great social stigma was placed on the first partner to leave the marriage (i.e. the cause of the break up). According to Mary, the marriage was on the rocks but neither wanted to be seen as the cause of the break up. Mary told the *North Shore Times*: "Shortly before my confinement he made me a definite offer of 15 shillings per week if I would live separately from him. This offer I declined, saying that, if we separated, he would have to leave first. About a week after the child was born, he came home much discontented, packed up his clothes, and said he was going off to leave me, going in an Orient steamer."[21]

If George had expected be a Victorian head-of-the-house after his marriage, he was sadly disappointed. At his trial, George tried to paint a picture of himself as a dutiful husband, but much put upon, while Mary complained of mental cruelty by him. In modern colloquialism, it was very much a "he said, she said" case.

Of course, as George had now been convicted of her attempted murder, Mary would now be eligible for a divorce, her husband being the guilty party.

A marriage, initially kept secret, was now being discussed and dissected Australia wide.

Part 2
Justice on Trial

It is better to let the crime of the guilty go unpunished than to condemn the innocent.
Justinian I
Law Code, 535 AD

To live in a land where justice is a game
The Hurricane by Bob Dylan

6.

Pickpockets and Thieves

> *The whole lot of us were in gaol twenty-five years ago last Christmas.*
>
> **Yorkie Bill**

The Dean Royal Commission opened on Monday, May 13, 1895, and met in the board room of the Colonial Secretary's office. The Government complied with William Trickett's demand, made at the Sydney Town Hall meeting, that they appoint three commissioners, one a prominent barrister and two highly respected medical men: Francis Edward Rogers QC, Dr Philip Sydney Jones and Dr Frederick Norton Manning (who had served on Büttner Royal Commission). At its initial meeting, Chairman Rogers stated that the Commission would sit on four weekdays, not Tuesdays, from 9:00 am to 5 pm, with an hour for lunch; the press and members of the Dean Defence Committee would be permitted to observe the proceedings.

Sir Julian Salomons QC and Charles Wade QC represented the Crown, and were intent on preserving the life sentence given to George Dean. In 1886, Salomons had been appointed Chief Justice, but resigned just a week later after receiving criticism of his appointment from other judges, particularly Windeyer – it was suggested in some quarters that their main objection to him was that he was Jewish. Wade was well acquainted with the case, having been the assistant prosecutor to Attorney-General Want at Dean's trial.

Justice on Trial

The Royal Commission consisted of chairman Francis Rogers QC (1841-1925), Dr Frederick Manning (1839-1903) and Dr Phillip Jones (1836-1918). Rogers was a leading barrister and, on occasion, an acting judge on the Supreme Court. Dr Manning had also served on the commission of inquiry into the Ernst Büttner case. Dr Jones was knighted in 1905 for his medical research. The doctors established that false evidence had been given in Dean's trial about the counter effects of arsenic and strychnine.

All witnesses were sworn in before giving evidence and, as in a trial, could be charged with perjury if found to be lying.

Charles Pilcher QC represented George Dean (paid by the Dean Defence Fund), assisted on some days by Dr R H Todd, a medico-barrister, and was instructed by Meagher. At the opening of the Commission proper on Wednesday, Pilcher indicated his main thrust: "In cases of poisoning where you cannot trace the purchase of poison, and where you have to rely upon the evidence of two women as to the administration of the poison, which is denied by the prisoner, it is of the utmost importance that the Commission, in dealing with the matter, should have as much light as possible thrown upon the characters of these three persons – Mrs Dean, Mrs Seymour and Dean himself."[1]

"The question is," Sir Julian said, "Who administered it [the poison]?"

"Exactly," Pilcher replied. "Our theory is, and I believe it will be shown beyond all question, that Mrs Dean has been an arsenic eater for years … for the purpose of improving her complexion and brightening her eyes. I believe it will be shown that arsenic eaters – men and women – have eaten on occasions as much as would kill a man."[2]

"I submit this is altogether irrelevant to the case," Salomons replied.

It was soon very clear that Caroline Seymour and daughter Mary Dean were the ones on trial at the Dean Royal Commission.

The Dean Royal Commission received depositions from a number of Melbourne policemen on Caroline Seymour's criminal career, which began at the Old Bailey (Central Criminal Court, London) on November 24, 1851 – she was charged with pickpocketing. John Oxenford deposed that he had been walking with Alice McKeller along a crowded London street, when they were crushed by two women who grabbed at his coat. Alice saw Caroline take Oxenford's gold watch, valued at £50; when she called out, the other woman fled. The Old Bailey recorded Caroline's name as Catherine Adams (although she always gave her given name in Australia as Caroline or Carrie); her age as twenty-one; and her place of origin as Kentish Town (north-west of London). She received a sentence of seven years transportation.[3]

Carrie Adams arrived in Hobart on board the *Sir Robert Seppings* on July 8, 1852. On May 2, 1853, she married John Asbury. He was aged nineteen when convicted at the Old Bailey of pickpocketing on April 3, 1848, and sentenced to

This newspaper portrayal of Caroline Seymour was based on a studio photograph. Other newspaper drawings in no way flattered her. She was convicted at the Old Bailey under the name Catherine Adams, became Caroline "Carrie" Ashbury after her marriage to John, changed to Caroline Gaynor while living with Denis Gaynor, and adopted Caroline Seymour after removing to Sydney.

On the right is one of a number of prison photographs of Denis Gaynor, Mary Dean's biological father – Mary's name at birth was Sarah Annie Gaynor. As a career thief, all too often caught, Gaynor spent many years in Victorian gaols and appears to have had no contact with his daughter.

seven years transportation (it was not his first conviction). A daughter, Caroline "Carrie" Asbury was born to the couple on May 24, 1854. By the end of 1865, Caroline had separated from John Asbury and moved to Melbourne. Aged sixteen in 1870, daughter Carrie married William Henry Brown, and gave birth to a son in 1872, named the same as his father. She appears to have died sometime in the 1870s.

John Asbury had joined the police force and risen to Sergeant by the birth of the baby Carrie (a shortage of free labour in Tasmania enabled convicts with good records to be part of the police force). He went into the hotel business in 1857. In Melbourne in 1869, then cohabiting with Winifred Dalwood (who bore him three children), he was convicted of assault and robbery and sentenced to three years in gaol. Dalwood migrated to New Zealand. In 1873, Asbury was convicted of housebreaking and, due to his previous convictions, received an eight year gaol sentence.[4]

Sarah Annie Gaynor was born on May 16, 1874 at Rosebank Cottage, Abbotsford Street, West Melbourne. Her birth certificate recorded her parents as Caroline Gaynor and Denis Gaynor and gave a wedding date, which later proved to be false. Although Caroline Asbury lived with Gaynor as his wife under his name, she never divorced John Asbury. At the time of the birth of his daughter, Denis Gaynor was serving a three-month gaol sentence. Following convictions for stealing in 1875 and 1879, Gaynor received gaol sentences of one year and three years, respectively.[5]

On February 13, 1877, Caroline Asbury was convicted at Collingwood Court of shoplifting two pairs of boots. As she had three previous convictions, she was sentenced to twelve months gaol, hard labour.[6] Following her release from gaol, Caroline seems to have determined to try and leave her criminal life behind her and removed to Sydney, renaming herself as Caroline Seymour, and renaming little Sarah Annie Gaynor as Mary "May" Ada Seymour.

In his written deposition, Superintendent Thomas O'Callaghan of the Victoria Police included the lines: "[Carrie Asbury] was the paramour for several years of Denis Gaynor, a well-known pickpocket. She was also the paramour of Jerry Scanlan, who was also a clever pickpocket … There were numerous convictions against Denis Gaynor and Scanlan

... I have seen Carrie Asbury taking men with her to brothels, and have afterwards seen the men, when they complained that she had bilked [cheated] them. During all the time I knew Carrie Asbury, she had the character of being a very dangerous and vindictive woman, one who would not stop at any crime to gain her object."[7]

Renting in Riley Street, Surrey Hills, for sixteen years or more, Caroline opened a boarding house initially and later incorporated a store at the front, leaving a life of crime behind her. She appears to have protected daughter Mary from the seedier side of her history. She made sure she went to school, where she made good progress, and also sent her for music lessons.

Pilcher QC called his first witness, William Ellis, generally known as "Yorkie Bill". The *Daily Telegraph* described Ellis as "a tall well-preserved individual with grizzled hair and particularly bright eyes" and a man whose career had been "devoted to crime".[8] Aged 67, Yorkie Bill was quite at ease in the witness box, even enjoying the spotlight, as he answered questions about his criminal career. Mrs Seymour was brought into the boardroom and he identified her as Carrie Asbury, who he had first met, thirty years ago, in Ballarat. That was not her maiden name; she had married a policeman named Jack Asbury. At Ballarat, she was not with her husband but with Denis Gaynor and Biddie Birch; they were picking pockets and shoplifting. And Carrie Asbury was "one of the smartest pickpockets who ever came to Australia".[9] He gave some examples of robberies committed by Carrie, Denis, Lizzie Footer and himself.

"I understand that ... [Mrs Seymour] was transported to

Pickpockets and Thieves

Two witnesses at the Royal Commission were William Ellis aka "Yorkie Bill", left, who seemed to enjoy his time before the Commission, and an aged Thomas Jones, who needed a crutch.

Tasmania for stealing a watch and that she has more than once been convicted in Victoria for pocket-picking or stealing, and that she was an associate of thieves and bad characters," Sir Julian conceded. "I will allow that she followed a criminal course up until the time she came to this colony [NSW]. But I deny, whatever her character is, that it has any bearing on this case."[10]

"Was Carrie Asbury in gaol in Melbourne?" Dick Meagher asked Yorkie Bill.

"Yes, the whole lot of us were in gaol twenty-five years ago last Christmas," Yorkie Bill replied, amid much laughter.

Yorkie Bill told the Commission he also knew Carrie when she came to Sydney sixteen years ago; she was living with a pickpocket name Billy Gamble. A detective named Williams pinched her for pickpocketing; Yorkie lent her money for a solicitor and she was acquitted. She also worked the pickpocket game with Tommy Jones. After that she became quiet; when he returned to Sydney fourteen years ago she was running a shop in Surrey Hills, selling fruits, lollies, cordials. He met men there who he knew to be criminals. He had last seen Carrie's other daughter twenty years ago; she was also called Carrie but she had since died.

Robert Hannan stated to the Commission he had worked as policeman in both Sydney and Melbourne. He had known Carrie Asbury in Melbourne as "a shoplifter, a pickpocket and an associate of thieves". He had last seen her twelve years ago in Newtown, Sydney – she was at a place kept by Yorkie Bill.[11]

Former policeman Philip Williams told the Commission he had reached the rank of First-class Detective with the Sydney Police before losing the job due to his drinking. Mrs Seymour was brought into the room and he identified her as Carrie Asbury.

"When I was in the police force," Williams declared, "I discovered her to be one of the cleverest women in Sydney … She was known as a woman who picked pockets and harboured thieves during the time that she lived in Norton Street."[12]

Williams also complained that Tommy Jones had assisted her pickpocketing operations, and had on occasions warned Carrie Asbury when he sighted the detective following her.

An aged Thomas "Tommy" Jones used a crutch and a walking stick to get to a seat before the Commission. He told Committee President Rogers he had been a tradesman – a tailor who had worked with the David Jones and Alfred Hordern companies at various times – never a criminal. He denied ever assisting Mrs Seymour in pickpocketing forays. When questioned on Caroline Seymour's past, Jones was very evasive; for someone who had known her for over forty years and boarded with her for fourteen years in Sydney, he knew so little about her.[13]

Did Jones know Mrs Seymour in Hobart?

Yes, but he did not know her name. He only knew her by sight, not to speak to.

Did he know her in Melbourne?

Yes, he had spoken to her there, but he knew nothing about her in Melbourne.

Had he lived with her in Sydney?

Yes, he had boarded with her for fourteen years, but had not lived with her (in a sexual sense).

Had anyone who had served a criminal sentence stayed with Mrs Seymour?

No, he never saw any.

Did Mrs Seymour ever go to Madame Rose's house?

Yes, she did, but Mary never went there.

Jones was currently living at the Liverpool Benevolent Asylum (in welfare accommodation). He admitted to Pilcher that Mrs Seymour had recently visited him at Liverpool, but denied she had requested him to tell the Commission he knew nothing about her troubled background. Pilcher forced Jones to admit that a criminal named Millet (aka Billy Gamble) had lived in a sexual relationship with Mrs Seymour, and had died at her boarding house.

The most sensational witness of the six-week Commission was a "decrepit old man"[14] who limped into the Commission room using a walking stick, and on being seated told the Commission President: "I am very ill. But in giving evidence I will speak the truth. I am nearly at death's door."[15]

Pilcher QC asked Caroline Seymour to be brought into the room.

Justice on Trial

In 1843, John Asbury was aged 14 when convicted at the Old Bailey (Central Criminal Court, London) of pickpocketing a handkerchief (worth three pence), and gaoled for three months. Two years later, he was convicted of the same offence and gaoled for six months. And in April 1848, aged 19, he was convicted a third time of pickpocketing a handkerchief, and transported for seven years.

"Do you know this woman now before the Commissioners?" Pilcher asked.

"Yes, that is my wife," the witness replied. He had not seen her for twenty-one years.

This witness was John "Jack" Asbury, aged 70. Caroline staggered out of the Committee room and fainted before she could reach the room reserved for waiting witnesses.[16] On the previous Saturday, Asbury said, a man had shown him a copy of the *Evening News*, and he was amazed to find his name in it. He subsequently went to North Sydney, and eventually contacted Mr Goddard on the Dean Defence Committee.

Asbury gave details of meeting and marrying his wife after they were both transported to the Tasmanian colony.[17] After serving in the police force, he had bought a series of hotels in Hobart. While he owned the Emu Hotel, his wife fled the colony, taking all the cash she could lay her hands on.

"On the 5th July, 1865, she left me," Asbury told Pilcher QC.

"Did she go away with any other person?"

"Not to my knowledge," Asbury replied. "She cleared out on a steamer named the Southern Cross, and went to Melbourne."

But she did not take their daughter Carrie with her. Little

Pickpockets and Thieves

The *Sunday Times* depicted the dramatic moment when an unsuspecting Caroline Seymour was brought into the courtroom to be identified by her estranged husband – she had left him thirty years before. Seated at the Commission table are John Pilcher QC, left, and Dick Meagher.

Carrie was about twelve at the time, and he put her into a boarding school. Four years later, in 1869, he moved to Melbourne and bought the Commercial Hotel in Bourke Street.

Did you send your daughter to boarding school while you were there?

"No … I kept her with me; I was so very fond of her."

"Did you see your wife in the Commercial Hotel?"

"Yes, on three different occasions."

"What became of the little girl?"

"One afternoon her mother rushed into the private bar, flourishing an umbrella, saying, 'You wretch, give me my child;

she shan't remain with you.' She took the child, got into a cab, and drove away."

"After that, did you do something towards the support and education of the child?"

"Yes, I paid £1 per week."

"Who came for the money?"

"The little girl, every Monday morning."

Asbury told the Commission of a terrible illness he once suffered while living with his wife at the Emu Hotel. The hotel had suffered a plague of rats. He bought some arsenic and, having received directions from the chemist for the amount of dosage, both he and wife set the baits. They were so successful, the hotel began to stink and they had to rip up the floorboards to remove dead rats. They were living happily at this stage.

Shortly afterwards, they had their first serious quarrel, although they had been having some minor squabbles before this. He became violently ill: "I was taken ill all of a sudden with pains inside – terrible pains inside – griping, vomiting, purging. They all came on at once. I said, 'My God! Ain't I bad!' And I was bad too. I went straight to the bedroom."

He sent a servant to get his wife: "[Carrie] came to the bedroom door and said, 'What's the matter?' I said to her, 'I'm in dreadful agony; bring me some brandy – for God's sake bring me some brandy.' She said, 'Oh, it's nothing,' and went back to the bar."

He was attended by both Dr King and Dr Agnew; he believed the latter was still living in Hobart. Pilcher asked what medical instructions were given to him by Dr Agnew.

Sir Julian Salomons became more and more agitated as he listened to Asbury's evidence. It was highly inflammatory against

Pickpockets and Thieves

Mrs Seymour, but no real proof of poisoning by arsenic was being offered; it could be described as hearsay at best. Asbury retired from the Committee room while Salomons and Pilcher had a heated debate over the admissibility of this evidence.

The *Truth* newspaper reported:[18] "In the course of the argument Sir Julian scornfully alluded to the public agitation on behalf of Dean as being '*factitious*' and as having '*been worked up*'."

"Send for Dr Agnew, send for him," Sir Julian demanded (and Agnew would be able to recall this particular case from thirty years ago?)

"It's all very well to say, 'Send for him'," said Pilcher. "Where's the money to come from? We haven't the Government behind us [paying for everything] like you have."

President Rogers permitted Pilcher to continue his line of questioning.

Asbury said Dr Agnew asked his wife to keep his vomit and purging so it could be examined, but she did not. When he next saw the bottle of arsenic, he notice that the cork had been put in differently than when he had used it last.

Then his wife tried to stab him.

On a Saturday, after returning to Hobart after a trip to New Zealand, he accused his wife of carrying on with another man while he was away. She flew into a violent temper. He said he would not discuss it any further then as the hotel was busy.

"Leave it till Monday," he had said to her. "If I am able to prove something [by] then, it will be God help you."

That night, as he was walking along Argyle Street with a policeman named MacGuire, someone wrapped in a cloak made a rush at him. MacGuire grabbed at the person and they rolled over and over on the ground – the hood went back to reveal it was his wife, and a knife fell from her hand. MacGuire told him he had "a narrow escape" and detained her while he went back to the hotel. But he decided not to charge her. On the following Monday she fled the colony.

In his closing testimony, Asbury claimed innocence of the crime for which he had spent two and half years in gaol – the theft of a fob watch.

Two days later, Sir Julian Salomons recalled John Asbury to the Commission hearing, and found it hard to get a straight answer out of him as the questioning descended into pure farce.

"Did you not, when giving evidence the other day," Sir Julian asked, "desire the Commissioners to understand that your wife had attempted to poison you?"[19]

"No," Asbury replied.

"What was the object of giving evidence at all then about the bottle and the cork being awry, or, at all events, it not being in the bottle the same way as you placed it there?" an astounded President Rogers interjected. "What did you give that evidence for?"

"I will tell you," Asbury replied. "In the first place to show that she and me both handled the poison, and, in the next place, to show that the cork of the bottle had been tampered with."

"I want to know what you gave that evidence for?" the President persisted.

"Because when I was buried in the bush at Paka Lakes Station, years after, I said to myself, 'My God, that woman tried to kill me when I was in the Emu Hotel'."

"Then do you mean to charge her with having attempted to poison you?" Sir Julian asked.

"I have my own thoughts," Asbury replied.

"And what are they?"

Pickpockets and Thieves

This *Bulletin* cartoon was captioned: "No names please!" One witness, who was examined by the Commission about Madame Rose, gave the name of a prominent politician as a visitor. The name was not recorded in the transcripts and other witnesses, when speaking about the brothel, were told: "No names please!" The Commissioners are seated behind the table. Charles Pilcher QC, for Dean, is at the end of the table, left, and Justice Sir Julian Salomons QC, for the Government, is on the other end of the table.

"After the Paka Lakes affair I did think so. When I was poisoned there."

"Was your wife there then?"

"No, but the symptoms were the same as those I had when at the Emu Hotel."

"How many years ago is that?"

"Five or six, I should think."

Asbury denied statements he made in his testimony to the Commission two days previously but, when the official record was read to him, he conceded he must have made them – he claimed he had a bad memory. This was a Royal Commission not a trial, and the Commissioners could afford to be much more tolerant with a witness than a trial judge, but their tolerance was certainly being severely tested.

"Mr Asbury, let me ask you this," Sir Julian said. "You remember that dagger scene you mentioned, when she attempted to stab you?"

"That was only a fizgig," Asbury replied. "I did not take it seriously."

"You did not take it seriously?"

"No, I did not think anything about it. I was not frightened. We slept together afterwards. What more can I tell you?"

"And you slept with her that night?"

"Yes."

Just a week into the Royal Commission, the weekly newspaper *Truth* provided a lengthy report of the Commission's proceedings, which included the following subheadings:[20] "Mrs Seymour's Character Blackened Beyond Judicial or Official Redemption" and "Dean's Character – More Testimony to Dean's Virtues". Wherever Caroline Seymour went and was recognised – particularly when she had to run the gauntlet of men gathered outside the parliamentary buildings each day of the Commission hearings – she was booed and hissed.

Those who came forward to give evidence about George Dean had nothing but praise for his character. Even police, who were involved in the case, commented favourably on his good character.

As well as the revelations of Caroline Seymour's criminal background, quite a number of witnesses were brought forward to say they had seen her entering Madame Rose's brothel. One witness told the Commission that Mrs Lee's house, where Caroline had gone after her eviction from the Dean house, was also a brothel. Later in the Commission hearings, Sir Julian brought forward many witnesses who stated that Caroline and her daughter had been nothing but good citizens as they ran

Pickpockets and Thieves

This savage sketch printed by *Truth* has Caroline Seymour proposing a toast: "May something happen to George Dean, so that I may get my poor girl back again!"

their shop in Surrey Hills.

In his opening address, Pilcher QC told the Commissioners that Mary Dean was an arsenic-eater, but at no stage did he produce any evidence to this effect. But he did offer the possibility that Mrs Seymour had tried to buy some arsenic. John Hall, a chemist in Surrey Hills, stated to the Commissioners that a constable came and asked him if George Dean had bought poison from him. He checked the poison book for the last two years and did not find the name there. He was shown a photo of a man, which he presumed to be George Dean, but could not recognise him.

The constable returned on another day and asked about a woman buying poison. There was only one such woman in the poison book and he gave him her description.

There was a lady who came to his shop some eight or nine months ago and asked for sixpence worth of arsenic. He told that

119

woman he could not sell her arsenic unless she had a witness who would verify her use of it. She had persisted in her demand for the arsenic, saying she wanted to kill rats and vermin; she only wanted a small amount, what she could buy for sixpence, and he need not put the chemist's label on it. But he refused to sell her any.

Sir Julian asked Hall if he had given the latter information to the constable.

"No," Hall replied, "I do not remember doing so."

Mr Meagher had shown him some photographs in his office, Hall said, and the one he picked out was Mrs Seymour. While he thought it was her, he was not prepared to swear it was her. Hall said he did not know much about the Dean trial as he had not been reading the papers (much to Sir Julian's astonishment). He had not volunteered this information to Crick and Meagher, they had sought him out; he did not know how they found out about it. He had previously run a business in Woollahra, and may have come in contact with George Dean, but was not aware that he had.

Mrs Seymour was brought into the Committee room: "Was this the woman?"[21]

"I would not swear that she was," Hall declared, "but it was a person very much after her style and manner. It would be a very remarkable coincidence if it were not."

A fortnight later, Hall again appeared before the Commissioners. Sir Julian cross-examined him intensely on the second occasion the constable (named Sutherland) visited him – and confusion reigned all round. Hall claimed he had mixed up the descriptions of the two women with the constable, the one in the book and the one he would not sell to – he could remember some conversations clearly but had no memory of others.

In answer to Pilcher QC, Hall said he had seen Mrs Seymour

before entering the Committee room and believed she was the woman, but he would not swear to it.

A week later, Senior-Constable William Sutherland deposed to the Commission that he visited Hall's pharmacy on March 14, and questioned Hall about George Dean buying poison. Hall checked his poison book but did not find Dean's name there.

"The face seems to me familiar," Hall had said, looking at the photo of George Dean, "but I cannot say that I know him."[22]

Sutherland said he returned to the shop on March 30 and read out a description of Mrs Seymour to Hall: "A woman about 53 years old,* 5 feet 7 inches tall [170 cm], medium build, dark hair turning grey, thin face, sallow complexion, walks very erect, and holds her head up; generally dressed in a black dress and small black bonnet"

"A woman of that description came to my shop some time ago," Hall said after pondering it for several minutes. "She wanted to purchase some strychnine. I refused to sell it to her as she had no witness."

Did Hall say she wanted strychnine, not arsenic?

Constable Sutherland was positive Hall had said strychnine; he had written it down.

Jane Reynolds deposed to the Commission that she was the wife of the publican at the Young Australia Hotel in Riley Street, Surrey Hills, near Madame Rose's. One morning, between 10:00 and 10:30, a woman came into the hotel "more drunk than sober", but able to walk. She did not know her at the time but had since identified her as Mary Dean, having been shown a photograph of her and recently taken to her ward in hospital.

---

* In fact, Caroline Seymour was aged 63.

This woman told her she was "the wife of a captain living at North Shore". She ordered a bottle of English ale and, after drinking some, went out the back to be sick. This woman told her she had been drinking wine all night at Madame Rose's and that caused her to be ill after drinking the ale – she then drank the rest of the ale. A cab waited outside the hotel while she was there, and she departed in it after about twenty minutes.[23]

In cross-examination by Sir Julian, Reynolds said there were no other witnesses – the woman was the sole customer at the time, and her hotel staff were elsewhere in the hotel.

When did Mrs Dean come to the hotel? About two months after her daughter's marriage – she married on October 26.

Was the woman eight or nine months pregnant?

"This person was loosely dressed at my place," Reynolds replied. "I would not say whether she was or was not. I cannot say."

This evidence by Jane Reynolds was simply unbelievable – was she unaware Mary had given birth on December 26?

On May 17, Mary Dean was transferred from the North Shore Hospital to Sydney Hospital, adjacent to the parliamentary buildings. By June 10, she was considered well enough to make the short walk, assisted by a nurse, to the Commission hearing. Once again she was taken through the evidence she had given at the committal hearing and the trial, giving much the same answers.[24]

But she was also examined on some bizarre new evidence.

Widow Margaret Parker told the Commission that she was a clairvoyant who went under the name of Madame Von. Mary Dean came to consult her on the Monday three days before George Dean's trial began. She asked Mary to take off her gloves and, after examining her hands, told her she was

A nurse accompanied Mary from Sydney Hospital – adjacent to the Parliamentary buildings – and sat beside her as she gave evidence to the Royal Commission.

married and that she had a child. Mary had denied both these statements to her.

"Did you look at her wedding ring?" President Rogers asked incredulously.[25]

"Oh, no!" Parker replied. 'We have signs that I can tell anything in that way … She had nothing on her fingers."

Parker said she told Mary she could see her husband, clairvoyantly; he was in gaol. Mary asked her if he would get out of gaol. She replied that Mary could get her husband out of gaol. Mary then said that if he got out, she would divorce him, that she hated him. Parker also told Mary that she could see a fair man, not her husband, in her future. Mary said, "That is the man I am going to marry." The session was interrupted by another client, who, on sighting Mary, told Madame Von that she was Mary Dean, the woman who accused her husband of poisoning her.

After Mary confessed she was indeed Mrs Dean, Parker claimed she asked Mrs Dean: "Won't you save your husband?"

"No, I hate him," Mrs Dean replied.

One could only doubt most of this evidence, yet it was reported in the newspapers as fact, amid much amusement, and had been read by Mary before arriving at the Commission. Mary admitted to the Commissioners that she had gone to

Madame Von for a consultation, paying her one shilling – she often visited clairvoyants. Curiosity was her reason; with the impending trial she wanted to know what would happen. During her visit, a woman, who knew her through the shop at Surry Hills, identified her to Madame Von.

But Mary completely denied the evidence given by Madame Von to the Commission.

"Can you tell me what questions she asked you," President Rogers asked Mary.[26]

"She asked me was I married. I said, 'Yes.' She said, 'You have two or three children,' and I said, 'No.' She said that if I was not careful, a dark woman would take my husband away from me. She said I was going to remove from where I was and go on a long journey."

"Anything else?"

"I do not think so."

"Fortune-tellers have told you something like that before?"

"Yes."

Sir Julian Salomons obtained the depositions taken at Narrandera in 1879 when George, aged twelve, was convicted of horse stealing and submitted them to the Commission – these would then appear among the documents printed in the Royal Commission's report.[27]

President Rogers stated that George's conviction was technically wrong – under the Act in 1879, only a judge and jury could convict someone of horse stealing, not a magistrate.[28]

"I would not like to be judged on what I did when I was 13," President Rogers added. "I do not think my colleagues will place much weight on this charge of illegally using a horse."[29]

Sir Julian admitted the horse stealing had no bearing on the poisoning case against George, but said he wanted to show that George was not the saintly character he had been painted before the Commission.

Charles Pilcher was absent from the Commission on this particular morning. In the afternoon, after a heated exchange with Pilcher, Salomons withdrew the depositions.

7.

Neighbours

I did not notice that it tasted different to any other tea.
Bessie Adey

The public outrage at the conviction of George Dean was caused by the role of the judge, Sir William Windeyer, and his handling of the case, yet this aspect was not to be examined by the Royal Commission – there was a great fear in the legal establishment of there being any official criticism of a judge, believing that such criticism could lead to a loss of faith in the justice system. This was despite the fact that the *Bulletin* newspaper, for one, had been castigating and lampooning Windeyer for several years.

There were no official records of trials in this period. Depositions were taken at committal hearings and these were sent to the Attorney-General's department for the sole purpose of determining whether or not to proceed to trial. At the trial itself, no depositions were taken and there was no official record of the statements made by the witnesses. Therefore the Dean Commission needed to rely on the Judge's Notes, written by Windeyer as the witnesses gave their evidence, as the only record of the trial's proceedings. Of necessity, over four long days of the trial, these could only summarise the evidence presented by witnesses which the Judge deemed important. The alternative was to resort to newspaper reports, but then there was a question of accuracy.

Appeals to the High Court could only be made on technical

issues; incorrect evidence given and accepted at a trial did not constitute any basis for an appeal.

The two medical Commissioners, Dr Sydney Jones and Dr Norton Manning, had been appointed specifically to examine all aspects of the alleged poisonings at the Dean trial. The evidence they received from William Hamlet, the Government Analyst, and the two doctors treating Mary Dean, Dr Newmarch and Dr Rennie, all indicated that they believed there was some counteraction between the two poisons arsenic and strychnine. Unable to find any current medical writing on the subject, the Commissioners contacted Dr Charles Martin, at the University of Sydney. He conducted exhaustive experiments on rabbits and submitted a report to the Commission, which detailed his experiments and answered the two basic questions asked by the Commission:[1]

- That arsenic was quite unable to mask the poisonous action of strychnine
- That when strychnine was introduced after arsenic, there was a small increase in blood pressure initially, but it was quite unable to counteract the arsenic.

Alexander and Catherine Weynton lived next door to the Deans in Miller Street, North Sydney, together with their four boys, the eldest being Oswin, aged eighteen. George was renting the Dean house from Alexander's brother. The two families did not socialise, other than to occasionally pass pleasantries over the fence. On April 25 (after Dean's trial was completed), Sub-Inspector Tindall and Constable Roche, acting on information received (but not revealing the source), went to the Weynton residence and dug in their backyard to find a bottle of strychnine.

Alexander deposed to the Commissioners that, in April

Neighbours

1894, his dog suffered badly from mange, and he asked Oswin to bring home some strychnine from his work so he could put the dog down – he then buried the dog in his backyard. This was four months before the Deans moved in next door.

Both Alexander and Catherine deposed that when they heard about the poisoning next door, they decided to bury the strychnine in the backyard – they said they were desperate not to be mixed up in the case. As police canvassed Miller Street residents, leading up to the trial, the Weyntons were able to answer honestly that there was no poison in their house.[2]

Oswin Weynton admitted to the Commission that he had brought the strychnine home from work but claimed that it had been given to him albeit unrecorded.[3] The firm later denied giving Oswin any strychnine and sacked him.

The Weyntons argued that this strychnine could not have been used in the poisoning of Mary Dean as it had been dyed pink[4] for commercial use. (But there was a high probability that, at the time of burying it, Alexander Weynton feared it could have been used to poison Mary.)

Catherine deposed that the only time Mary Dean came to her house was on Saturday morning, March 2, about 7:30, asking about the baby who "had a sort of convulsive fit". She suggested a bath, and they bathed Florence together in the Dean house.[5]

Mary appeared to be in her usual good health. Mary told her she had been vomiting but said nothing about lemon syrup cordial – and Mary did not vomit while she was there. Catherine did not see Mary again until Monday night. Around six o'clock, Catherine made up the baby's bottle and then stayed at the Dean house until ten o'clock. When the doctor came, Mary did not tell him anything about the lemon syrup. After the doctor left, Mary then told her about it, and she scolded

Mary for not telling the doctor. She told her husband about the lemon syrup, and he buried the strychnine early next morning.

Charlie and Annie Thompson lived two doors away from the Deans, on the other side of the Weynton residence. Charlie was also the engineer on the *Possum* with George, and they usually walked home together each morning after docking the *Possum* for the day. On the day Dean was arrested, Alexander Weynton had told Charlie about burying the strychnine in his backyard, but Charlie and Annie had kept that information to themselves when questioned by the police.

Charlie told the Commission he borrowed George's bike at midday on Saturday, March 2, and returned it two hours later. He spoke to Mary Dean on both occasions as George was out somewhere. That night he went to their house to speak with George about his own bike; he also spoke to Mary. On each occasion she seemed quite healthy.[6]

On the following Monday afternoon about five o'clock, he had borrowed George's bike to go and play cricket. George came running down to the oval and said: "I will take the bicycle Charlie. I want to go to Dr Newmarch. The missis is that bad I can't stand it anymore."[7] George returned with the bike about twenty minutes later.

The next morning, Tuesday, about eight o'clock, George came to his house; he was crying.

"For God's sake go down to the doctor's for me," George said, "my wife is awfully bad. There is no one inside to look after the child. Mrs Weynton was there but she has gone home. They are talking something about a bottle with poison in it."

Charlie fetched the doctor.

Annie Thompson told the Commission that while her husband went for the doctor she stayed with the Deans for several hours; it

Neighbours

was the first time she had been inside their house.

She took the baby from George and washed it. George was very kind to Mary, bathing her head with vinegar and water. At no stage did Mary vomit or purge.

Mary wanted some tea. George objected, saying it was against Dr Newmarch's directions, but Mary insisted.

"Oh, George! I will not get better," Mary cried after drinking the tea. "You'll have the baby. She will be good to you." [8]

"Oh! Don't say that," George cried.

After saying this, Annie said, George broke down completely and cried.

When the doctor came, he admonished Mary for having tea against his instructions.

Bessie Adey* provided compelling new evidence to the Commission about the strychnine-laced tea. On the Sunday morning (March 3), Mary had claimed her tea tasted bitter and she sent George to get Bessie, as a means of getting George out of the room while she hid most of the tea under a chest of drawers.

Bessie told the Commission it was about 10:30 am when she arrived in Mary's bedroom.

"When she was in bed," Pilcher QC asked, "did she look ill?"[9]

"No, she didn't look ill," Bessie replied. "She said she had a very bad headache."

"Is that all she complained of?"

"Yes."

"Whilst you were in the house on that Sunday ... did anything occur?"

---

* The reports of the Royal Commission misspelled her surname as Adye.

"She had a cup of tea and some toast beside the bed," Bessie replied. "She said Mr Dean had brought it up to her. I said, 'Why don't you drink it, it will do your head good?' She said, 'I do not like it; I got out of bed and put part of it away.' She asked me to taste it."

"Did you taste it?"

"Yes. I took a mouthful of it."

"Did you notice anything the matter with it?"

"I detected nothing wrong with it."

"Did you see any cream of any kind, or any white stuff around the edges," the President asked, "anything white at all?"

"No, Sir."

"You said it was all right?"

"Yes."

"When you tasted that cup of tea," Pilcher asked, "was there any bitter taste about it? Had it any taste foreign to it whatever?"

"No, none whatever."

"Did you take a good mouthful of it?"

"Yes."

"And did you swallow it?"

"Yes."

"And you were not ill?"

"Oh, no."

"You are quite certain of that, Mrs Adey?"

"Yes, I am quite sure."

Baby Florence was crying on the bed, so she took her back to the shop with her – her daughter Ethel looked after her – and returned Florence around 4:30 that afternoon. Mary was in bed; she looked the same as in the morning; she had colour in her face.

Bessie also revealed that Mary had visited her shop around 11:00 am, the next morning (Monday, March 4), seeking a bottle of soda water. Up until this point, it was generally believed that Mary had been too ill to get out of bed on this day. Mary had stayed about ten minutes, Bessie said. She complained of feeling faint and lay down for a few minutes. Bessie had no soda water and was awaiting a drink delivery. She sent four bottles of it down to Mary, via a little girl from next door, after it arrived later in the day.

Sir Julian Salomons made it clear in his cross-examination that he did not believe any of this testimony by Bessie.[10]

You were a witness at Dean's trial, Sir Julian demanded, why did you not give this evidence then?

"They never asked me if I had tasted the tea," Bessie replied. "… I answered the questions they asked me."[11]

But Charles Wade QC (who was assisting Sir Julian at the Commission and had also assisted Prosecutor Want at the trial) asked you outside the courtroom whether you had tasted the tea, Sir Julian continued.

"Yes, he did," Bessie replied. "He asked if I tasted the tea and I said yes."

"Did he ask you anything else about the tea?"

"Yes. He asked me what it tasted like and I said I did not notice that it tasted different to any other tea."

"On your oath will you swear that you did not tell him that you had not tasted the tea?" Sir Julian persisted.

"I did not tell him that I had not tasted the tea," Bessie replied.

"Just reflect for one moment. Will you not admit that?"

"No, Sir, I will not."

A week later Sir Julian called his assisting counsel, Charles Wade QC, as a witness and asked him if he had heard the evidence Mrs Adey gave to the Commission.

"I heard what she said about the tea," Wade replied.

"Is that true?"

"No, it is not."

"Why did you not ask [Mrs Adey] that at the trial?" Pilcher cross-examined.

"I think you will see from the Judge's Notes," Wade replied, "that an objection [by Mr Meagher] was taken when I wanted to ask that question."

This was not true – while Meagher may have objected at this point in the trial, Judge Windeyer's notes did not record it. The Judge recorded Bessie as stating she tasted the lemon syrup on the Saturday and found it tasted bitter. Windeyer then wrote: "I saw prisoner next day at 10:30. He asked me to come and see his wife, as she was very ill. I went to her. She was in bed. She had a cup of tea by the bed, about half a cup. Her face was flushed. We had a talk. I took the baby away home."

Four days later, Mary Dean appeared before the Commission and was questioned on Bessie's new evidence.

"What did you say to Mrs Adey [on that Sunday morning]?" President Rogers asked Mary.[13]

"That Mr Dean brought me some tea and toast," Mary replied.

"Did she taste it?"

"Yes, she did. She sipped it."

"And she noticed nothing wrong with it?"

"She said there was no taste whatever."

"Are you sure?"

"Yes, positive. She said it tasted all right."

"Did she tell you it was all right and ask you, 'Why don't you drink it?'?"

"No, she did not say that."

"Did she take a good sip?"

"No, she put the cup to her lips and sipped it."

"Did she take a mouthful?"

"I do not know."

Turning to Mrs Adey's evidence about the Monday morning, Dr Manning asked Mary: "Did you stay in your room all that Monday?"[14]

"No."

"You went out?"

"Yes."

"Where did you go?"

"To Mrs Adey's."

"What did you go to Mrs Adey's for?"

"To tell her I was ill."

Hans Bach told the Commission he spent the Monday in question with George, arriving at his house around 8:00 am. Hans, who had worked as a butcher for the Konnecke family over a number of years, met George about nine years ago when George was working for Mr Chadwick, a saw-miller in Liverpool Street; this was just before George went to work for the ferry company. Hans had recently fallen out with Mr Konnecke and was starting work at a different firm. He had reported at his new work on this particular Monday, but found he was not to start until the following Monday, and decided to go and see George.[15]

The main tenor of the evidence given by Hans was of George being a very good husband. George cooked breakfast downstairs and took Mary's breakfast up to her on a tray – two chops, bread and butter, and a cup of tea. Hans was also served breakfast, chops, steak and tea (from the same pot as Mary's tea). After breakfast, he helped George to wash the dishes and sweep out the rooms. George washed Florence in a basin, and dressed her, including a clean nappy. He also fed her from a bottle. Hans then nursed Florence until she went to sleep. Later George went to the shop for some groceries and cooked dinner. In the afternoon, George had a nap and farewelled Hans some time later.

Hans confirmed that Mary had left the house for around fifteen minutes in the morning. He also stated that, shortly after his arrival, George had taken him upstairs to Mary's bedroom to say hello to her. While he was in the bedroom, Mary began breast-feeding Florence. In her evidence to the Commission, Mary denied that Hans had been upstairs at any time during Monday, and she never breast-fed Florence on that day. Also, she was the one who washed and dressed Florence upstairs.[16]

On Wednesday, June 12, the Royal Commission began winding up. Both Salomons and Pilcher gave lengthy closing addresses to the Commissioners lasting a day and a half. On Friday, George Dean was taken from his Darlinghurst cell to make a brief appearance at the Royal Commission. The Commissioners stated that he was not there to be questioned, but he was free to make statements in his defence if he so desired – it was entirely voluntary on his part.

The main point made by George concerned the conversation between Dr Newmarch and himself about putting powder in Mary's medicine. At the trial, George said it occurred on Thursday while Dr Newmarch said it was Wednesday (and the Doctor was believed). To the Commissioners, Dr Newmarch had admitted he was in error at the trial, the conversation had occurred on the Thursday.

The last hearing was on the following Friday, when Bessie Adey was again recalled. Following a brief questioning, two cups of tea were presented to her in an experiment. President

Rogers wanted Bessie to taste the tea in each cup, stating the three Commissioners had already tasted them.

"Does that tea," Rogers asked after she tasted the first cup, "taste to you like the tea you tasted that morning at Dean's home?"[17]

"Yes," Bessie replied.

She baulked at tasting the second cup.

"You need not be afraid, Mrs Adey," Dr Manning reassured her, "it will not harm you."

"I do not like it," she said, after tasting it.

"Did you notice anything peculiar about the taste of the second cup of tea?" the President asked.

"Yes, it was very bitter."

"Did you notice a taste like that after the tea on that Sunday morning?"

"No, Sir."

The first cup was an ordinary cup of tea whereas the second contained one-fifteenth of a grain of strychnine, sufficient to provide strychnine's bitter taste, but insufficient to cause a nauseous reaction.

Mary Dean had sworn at Dean's trial that the tea she had on that Sunday morning tasted bitter, yet here was Bessie Adey swearing that it did not. And Mary confirmed to the Commission that Bessie had "sipped" the same cup of tea and said at the time that it tasted "all right".

Bessie Adey was the last of over a hundred witnesses to give evidence at the Dean Royal Commission, which took evidence on twenty-one sitting days over six weeks – the transcripts recorded 12,564 questions and answers. The three Commissioners retired to consider the evidence presented to them, and to write a report of their findings for the Government.

As all of Australia awaited the declaration of the report in eager anticipation, the *Daily Telegraph* interviewed seven of the jurymen who had convicted George Dean. All said that if they had heard the evidence presented to the Royal Commission, which they read in the newspapers, they would have declared Dean "not guilty".[18]

8.

Justice Demands

> *Dean's guilt or innocence is possibly even now a matter of conjecture. But justice does not act on conjecture. Justice demands that, before a man is imprisoned, his guilt should be proven.*
>
> **Editorial, The Bulletin**

On Friday morning, June 28, the Commissioners presented their report to the Government. The report itself (apart from the minutes, transcripts and accompanying documentation) consisted of four pages and was in two sections.

The two medical Commissioners, Dr Jones and Dr Manning, signed the first section.

They noted the "peculiar dangers" of taking evidence during the hearings, considering that the original evidence given at the trial had been so widely read, and the evidence given to the Commission could be "manufactured" or given a "special bias". But having been shown the criminal character of Mrs Seymour, they could only "regard her evidence with the gravest suspicion". As Mrs Dean had been reared "in such an unwholesome atmosphere" they had to view her evidence "with extreme caution" unless it could be corroborated by reliable witnesses. They took into consideration that Mr Westgarth gave evidence of Dean questioning him about divorce.

The medical Commissioners found that that Dr Martin's report confirmed their own view that "there had been no symptoms of poisoning by strychnine during Mrs Dean's illness, and no trustworthy evidence that strychnine had been taken." She had been poisoned by arsenic, but it may have only been one dose.

On Saturday, March 2, the symptoms of poisoning by arsenic in the lemon syrup rested "only on her assertion" and seemed "incompatible with her appearance and condition on that day as vouched for by several witnesses, and her action in walking a considerable distance and interviewing several neighbours."

Mrs Dean confirmed that on Sunday, March 3, Mrs Adey had tasted, or sipped, the tea, some of which she secreted under a chest of drawers, and had stated it tasted all right (not bitter as stated by Mrs Dean).

Mrs Dean had left the house around 11:00 am on Monday, March 4, after claiming to be vomiting and purging from an intake of arsenic at 9:00 am – this was completely new evidence. They did not believe that such a person could have the "ability or inclination" to go out just two hours later. Further: "The consideration of all the evidence in detail with regard to this day induces a doubt as to whether the arsenic was taken in the morning at all, and inclines us to believe Dean's statement with regard to the events of this day, and that of other witnesses rather than those of his wife."

The two Commissioners stated that their attention was drawn to "Mrs. Dean's very peculiar conduct" where:
- She repeatedly took food and drink from her husband, although she admitted she was able to help herself, and, at the same time, she believed he was poisoning her.
- She did not convey her suspicions to her neighbours or friends with whom she had free contact.
- She refused to have medical aid on Sunday and Monday,

March 3 and 4, until her husband fetched the doctor without her consent. She then concealed information as to the cause of her illness from the doctor.

In the final paragraphs, they concluded: "We hold that the facts as shown are quite as compatible with the hypothesis that Mrs Dean, for reasons which we can only surmise, and by methods of which she has cognisance, administered the arsenic to herself – possibly at the prompting of her mother, and without any intention of taking a fatal dose … We have grave doubts if George Dean committed the offence with which he was charged, and of which he was found guilty, and we therefore recommend that he be released from further imprisonment."

In the second section of the report, President Francis Rogers signed his dissenting view: "There is apparently no escape from the position that this poison was either administered by Dean or by Mrs Dean herself. There are no doubt numberless contradictions and difficulties in the case, but … it seems to me unreasonable to suppose that a girl on the threshold of life (whatever may have been her early surroundings) would risk her existence by taking a deadly irritant poison, whether in one or more doses, for the purpose of bringing a false charge against her husband, and for this reason I cannot concur in the recommendation."

The Dean Royal Commission recommended by a 2-1 majority that George Dean be released from gaol.

And the question of who poisoned Mary Dean had largely been left unanswered. Two of the Commissioners believed there was a possibility she poisoned herself while the third believed this to be an unreasonable proposition.

The July edition of the *Australian Medical Journal* stated:[1] "The presence of medical men on the Commission was so valuable. The facts stated by the medical witnesses for the Crown were true enough as far as they went – that arsenic depresses the heart, and strychnine strengthens it, that arsenic generally is a depressant, and strychnine generally is a tonic, and so on – and a judge and jury might have been misled into believing that such a degree of antagonism would account for the absence of symptoms of strychnine poisoning. But the medical members of the Commission were not so misled, and to be perfectly certain, had experiments made by Dr Martin which conclusively proved that such a view as that advanced by the Crown was quite inadmissible ... It was equally clear that she was not poisoned by the contents of the bottle of lemon syrup which contained almost as much strychnine as arsenic [1½ grains of strychnine, 1¾ grains of arsenic]. Admitting that Mrs Dean was poisoned, the question of who poisoned her was one purely of probabilities ... there was not sufficient reliable evidence to make it most probable even that George Dean administered the poison. The case still remains to a large extent a mystery."

Having received the Royal Commission report in the morning, Premier Reid took it to the afternoon meeting of the Executive Council. After a full discussion, the decision was taken to release George Dean. A courier was rushed to the Governor, Sir Ralph Darling, who was leaving for Katoomba on the afternoon train, to sign Dean's release warrant – part of the prerequisite red tape needed for such a prisoner release – so Dean need not spend another night in gaol. Late in the afternoon, the announcement was made to the waiting reporters.

Thursday's newspapers had printed that a decision on George Dean would be made on this Friday, and people began gathering outside Darlinghurst Gaol gate at midday in the expectation of a positive declaration.

Dick Meagher visited George in his cell during the afternoon. "Don't be too certain of getting out," Meagher said. "I think it is all right, but you can't be sure. So do not make up your mind that you are going to be a free man."[2]

George received no further news and, on the gaol "lights out" at seven o'clock, he hopped into bed. Half an hour later, he was woken by Senior-Warder Barrie.

"Put these on, George," the warder said, holding a light and tossing street clothes into the cell. "You are a free man."

He was taken to the office of the Gaol Governor. There, together with Governor Herbert, were members of the Dean Defence Committee – among them Robert Moodie, William Evans and Fred Konnecke. Everyone jubilantly shook hands with him.

"Knowing I was an innocent man," George said, "I did not think I would get into the whole trouble, but at times I was despondent."

By this time hundreds of people (one newspaper even estimated 5,000) surrounded the main gate of the gaol, hoping to get a glimpse of him leaving the gaol. Instead George was escorted along an underground passage to a different exit where a cab was waiting.[3] Ironically, this was the same passageway used to convey him from the courtroom to the gaol death cell, after his conviction and sentencing by Judge Windeyer.

George was taken to the committee room of the William Evans company in Hunter Street, the headquarters of the Dean Defence Committee. This Committee had worked so hard for George's release, raising money, organising meetings to secure the Royal Commission, and then, during the Commission hearings, seeking witnesses to support their case, and taking them to Meagher's office to make depositions and to appear before the Commission. George told the Committee he was only now beginning to learn what they had done for him as he had been in isolation in gaol, not permitted to talk to anybody, and receiving no newspapers. The Committee asked only one thing of George: to be conservative in his reactions to the vast popularity he would now encounter on his release. This he did, restraining his jubilation to smiling and shaking hands, and making no comments whatever about his wife, mother-in-law or Judge Windeyer.

Interviewed by a reporter in the Evans committee room, George was asked his future plans.

"I am going back to my old foster father," George said, "and I am never going to leave him again. He is my best friend."[4]

George left the meeting with Fred Konnecke and returned to the Woollahra residence, where he was joyfully welcomed back into the Konnecke family to resume permanent residence there.

The next morning, George crossed to the North Shore and met with Captain Summerbell, organising to return as ferry captain of the *Possum* on the following Wednesday night. All the company's boats were tooting and flying decorations in honour of George. Wherever he went, people wanted to shake his hand and congratulate him. Newspapers took photographs of him, and advertised them for sale. Offers, as much as the enormous sum of £100, were made for him to give lectures at meetings, but George refused them all.[5]

George did accept an offer from Alderman David Davis, chairman of the Dean Defence Committee, to accompany him to his country residence at Wentworth Falls in the Blue

Justice Demands

Mountains for a holiday. They left on the Saturday afternoon train and returned on Tuesday morning.

Newspaper editorials were full of praise for the majority decision of the Royal Commission, highly critical of Justice Windeyer and somewhat critical of the investigating police.

Much praise was heaped on Dick Meagher and Paddy Crick. Ernst Büttner had set the precedent for George Dean. His case had often been cited in the public meetings demanding the Dean Royal Commission. The parallels between the two cases of George Dean and Ernst Büttner were unmistakable: both men had been convicted and sentenced to hang; both had their convictions overturned and received free pardons; Crick and his legal firm (Meagher leading in the Dean case) had defended both men; Crick had harangued parliament, pleading the innocence of both men, leading to the eventual overturning of their convictions.

The newspapers also noted that it was not enough to release George Dean, he also needed to have full civil rights restored to him, and this could only be done with a free pardon which was duly issued, signed by Governor Darling.* On his return from the Blue Mountains, George attended the penultimate meeting of the Dean Defence Fund to receive a formal welcome back. They stated that his friend Harry Paul had been one of their hardest workers. For as long as he lived, George declared, he would never forget the work of this committee, Mr Meagher and Mr Crick.

---

* Some called this a "royal pardon" as it was signed by the Governor – as was the pardon received by Ernst Büttner – and free pardons were usually signed by the Colonial Secretary only. A "free pardon" overturned the conviction. Many convicts received a "conditional pardon", given on the condition they remained in the colony and did not return to Great Britain.

Later that night, George attended a function organised for him by the Masters and Engineers of Harbour and River Steamers' Association, of which he had been a member for some years. The Association had donated £100 to the Dean Defence Fund.

"If there had been any doubt as to Dean's innocence," the chairman declared, "it must have been removed in the case of all fair-minded men by the evidence brought before the Royal Commission."[6]

Following the cheering and applause, George once again proffered his thanks to all concerned.

On Wednesday night he resumed duty as skipper on the *Possum*. At the Lavender Bay wharf, his first stop to pick up passengers, fellow employees of the ferry company gathered to cheer him as the *Possum* departed, and were supported by the passengers, many of whom were riding the ferry especially to see George. At Circular Quay, many of his friends were there to cheer him and shake his hand. Later in the week, he was reported as having been seen riding his bicycle home from work early on a cold winter morning – he rode the length of Oxford Street with both hands in his pockets keeping them warm.[7]

On Friday night, July 12, a final function for George was put on by his fellow employees at the North Shore Ferry Company.

In the weeks that followed, things began to settle down into a normal routine.

George, as one newspaper phrased it, was promoted "marsupially"[8] from the *Possum* to the *Wallaby*, which steamed between Circular Quay and Mosman. This was a daytime steamer, one he had sought long before his arrest – no more night work.

William Finch, George's younger half-brother, made contact and was welcomed as a boarder alongside George in the Konnecke household.[9]

In the second week of July, amid the celebrations of George's release, it was reported that Mary Dean had returned to Sydney from the Camden Convalescent Home, to which she had been transferred after her appearance before the Royal Commission.[10]

Following George's conviction in April, Mary had no means of support. When first arrested, he gave permission for her to take the fob watch and about £3 removed from his pockets by gaol warders. Later, she wrote to him in gaol requesting written permission to access his bank account, but received no reply.[11] This left Mary with little option other than to reunite with her mother as she had before her marriage. The Miller Street house was vacated and Caroline Seymour returned to Surry Hills to open a shop in Little Collins Street, caring for baby Florence during Mary's hospitalisation.

While George was convicted of her attempted murder, Mary could divorce him. With the issue of his free pardon, George was no longer a convicted criminal, and the grounds for a divorce, by either party, disappeared. As one newspaper pointed out: "The case brought to light the strange fact that Mrs Dean can still claim all the rights and privileges of George Dean's wife, and that he cannot claim a divorce … Whatever the facts of the sad domestic tragedy, Mr and Mrs Dean cannot be ever again to one another as man to wife … But the law will wait until one of the pair sins against the marital contract, and only then will grant them liberation."[12] And the most common divorce sin was adultery.

But Mary could sue for maintenance. On September 17, her warrant for maintenance by George came before Stipendiary Magistrate Delohery at the Paddington Police Court. Several hundred people rushed the public seating, which became overcrowded, forcing a large overflow into the hall and outside the court building – all wanting to witness the exchange between the estranged husband and wife. It was apparent that Mary was fully restored to health. Fred Konnecke and other friends sat behind George, while Caroline Seymour nursed Florence behind Mary.

Paddy Crick, representing George, stated his client had not deserted his wife (meaning the split was mutual) but still wished to pay maintenance; it was simply an issue of how much. His client had not been earning money for some months – smiles went all around the courtroom – but he was now back at work earning £3 per week. His was paying off his debts, which had accumulated to £30, and could only afford to pay 10 shillings (£1 = 20 shillings) per week.

William Taylor, representing Mary, stated his client originally wanted £1 – two maintenance warrants had originally been issued, one for Mary and one for Florence, but the latter had been withdrawn before the court sat – but she would now accept 15 shillings.

"The child is really in a delicate state of health and is a great expense to the mother," Taylor said. "She thinks 15 shillings is barely sufficient."

"You can't take the child into consideration," Crick said. "Dean, as a matter of fact, is anxious to keep the child. He wishes to place it with some friends who are willing to adopt it."

Obviously this was the Konnecke family, but this was not the court to make such a determination.

After further haggling, the maintenance was settled at 12½ shillings per week, to be picked up from the Paddington Police Station each Monday. After six months, Mary could re-apply for a new determination.

The withdrawal of the warrant for Florence's maintenance

indicated Mary's fear she could lose Florence to George. It was usual for the mother to gain custody of the children following a marriage break-up, but perhaps Mary had been advised that the exposure of her mother's criminal career at the Royal Commission – and she was now living with her mother again – might threaten her custody, and prove the exception.

"Immediately Dean left the court," the *Australian Star* reported, "he rushed in the direction of his wife, and, snatching up the child, kissed it passionately."[13]

It was apparent that this was the first occasion on which George had held Florence since his arrest in March.

Outside the court, Mary and her mother suffered some booing from the crowd. A few of the crowd then followed them down the street, and continued the booing until they boarded a tram at the corner.[14]

The Australian population had avidly followed the case in the newspapers and, for the vast majority, the Royal Commission evidence proved that George did not poison Mary. This was quite false in that the Commission only found that there was insufficient proof that he poisoned Mary i.e. there was reasonable doubt – and certainly there was insufficient proof that she poisoned herself.

As a *Bulletin* editorial pointed out:[15] "Dean's guilt or innocence is possibly even now a matter of conjecture. But justice does not act on conjecture. Justice demands that, before a man is imprisoned, his guilt should be proven; and Dean's guilt has never been proven."

So the question remained.

Who poisoned Mary Dean?

9.

A Bruised Ego

The ego is not master in its own house.

Sigmund Freud

A general election had been called for the end of July, and Dick Meagher decided to stand for the seat of Sydney-Phillip against the sitting member, Alderman Fowler. Meagher was a Protectionist (in favour of import restrictions to protect local industries and opposed to the Free Traders) and with the Opposition. During the election campaign, the *Daily Telegraph* favoured the Government's campaign and, though it had once been so supportive of Dick Meagher, published an article criticising his handling of the Dean case: "Mr Meagher, whose failure to expose the singularly weak case against George Dean, put the country to the expense of a Royal Commission …"[1]

During the campaign, Premier Reid had received some flack about his reluctance to form the Dean Royal Commission and his Government's opposition to the overturning of Dean's conviction. At an election rally in Newcastle, the Premier followed the *Telegraph*'s line and criticised Dean's defence lawyers, declaring that "the praise Messrs Crick and Meagher had got for getting Dean off, after neglecting his first defence [trial], sickened him".[2] Crick and Meagher immediately issued a writ claiming £2,000 in damages against the Premier as a campaign ploy and never followed it up after the election.

Although Reid's Government won a resounding victory, Dick Meagher was victorious in Sydney-Phillip, and joined Paddy Crick on the Opposition benches.

But Meagher still fumed over the *Telegraph*'s criticism of him, and decided to seek the legal advice of Justice Sir Julian Salomons as to the possibility of suing the newspaper for defamation. Certainly Sir Julian had opposed him at the Royal Commission, but he was an eminent authority in jurisprudence, and his office was next door to the Crick legal office.

Early in August, Justice Sir William Windeyer again became involved in controversy. Twelve months previously, he had presided over a divorce case in which Richard Butler sued his wife Mary for divorce on the grounds of her adultery. Mary denied committing adultery and counter charged her husband with adultery, naming Widow Caroline Copp, his employer in a chemist shop, as the correspondent. She also claimed her husband physically assaulted her on several occasions. Butler produced an incriminating letter which he claimed was written by his wife, and which she claimed to be a forgery. John Johnson, Mary's brother, gave evidence that, about four years previously, he had come across Richard Butler in a compromising position with an unknown woman. Butler produced two witnesses who claimed to have witnessed Mary in a compromising position.

Windeyer granted the divorce stating he completely disbelieved the wife and her brother and castigated both of them severely. He ordered Mary out of the court, gave custody of their child to the husband and then ordered Johnson to be charged with perjury. In December, Johnson was convicted of perjury and given a sentence of three years. Johnson's

A Bruised Ego

A newspaper sketch shows Charles Williams diving under a table as Richard Butler confronts his wife in the contrived set-up. On the right is Charles Davis, aka Charles Williams, standing trial charged with conspiracy.

evidence about Butler revolved around Butler's ownership of a horse and cart, and Butler was able to establish he did not own the horse at that time.

Following Johnson's imprisonment, private investigations on Mary's behalf resulted in Richard Butler, Charles Davis (who had used the surname of Williams during the divorce proceedings) and his de facto wife, Elizabeth Peake, being charged with conspiracy to pervert the course of justice. At the divorce hearing, Butler had claimed he did not know Davis, but Davis' account books showed payments to him by Butler through his solicitor Thomas Rofe. The incriminating letter was proved to be a forgery by experts. Mary Butler said that on the night in question, Davis knocked on her door and she let him in. Shortly afterwards, as they were talking, Butler came home and Davis dived under a table as he entered the room; Butler and Davis then pretended to have a fight. Mary Butler went down on her knees to her husband and swore

153

to God she had done nothing wrong. All three accused were found guilty; Butler and Davis each received seven years, Peake three years.

Sensationally, Thomas Rofe was arrested at the completion of the trial and charged with conspiracy to pervert the course of justice. He had represented Richard Butler in the divorce case and, clearly, must have been aware of the falseness of the case against Mary Butler, even making payments to Davis on Butler's behalf. Dick Meagher obtained bail for him, and Paddy Crick represented him at the committal hearing, which opened on August 21, 1895. Crick stated that there was no doubt that the three people convicted of conspiracy were indeed guilty, but Rofe was just a lawyer taking instructions from his client (Butler). Rofe was committed to stand trial and found guilty. Justice Backhouse sentenced him to be gaoled for seven years but then suspended the sentence under the First Offenders Act, saying Rofe was a young man (aged 25) and an inexperienced lawyer. Rofe left the court a free man.

At the same time, a judicial enquiry was held into the conviction of John Johnson. With Johnson admitting he had lied about Butler's horse – but not about Butler's adultery – the Executive Council decided to let him serve out his sentence. Following continued rumblings in the press, Johnson was quietly released from gaol in the following February, having served 14 months of his three year sentence.

Once again, Justice Windeyer had adopted a view in a case and not content with simply expressing it – in this case by awarding the divorce to Richard Butler – he abused Mary Butler and ordered her out of the courtroom. And she was completely innocent.

A Bruised Ego

There was a notice of a motion before the House of Assembly to censure Justice Windeyer for his actions as a consequence of this case:

1. That, in the opinion of this House, his Honour Sir William Windeyer should no longer retain his seat as a puisne judge of the Supreme Court of New South Wales.
2. That the above resolution be communicated by address to his Excellency the Lieutenant-Governor.

But the Government wanted no part of it and continually deferred any discussion on the issue. Premier Reid claimed it was not an appropriate motion for the House and he referred it to the Crown Law Office (who, as expected, did nothing).[3]

On September 18, the day after George and Mary settled their maintenance issue in court, the report of the Dean Royal Commission was laid on the table in the House of Assembly, publishing the complete report and accompanying documentation for the first time.

On the same day, an astounding question was asked in the Legislative Council.

"Is there any foundation for the rumour that the Attorney-General has received a communication respecting an admission of guilt alleged to have been made by George Dean?" Henry Kater asked Attorney-General John Want. "Does the Attorney-General believe in the truth of the communication, and, if so, will he give the House the particulars of it?"[4]

"I regret I cannot answer the question," Want replied. "I have not received any communication which I can disclose in any shape or form."

Kater gave notice he would again ask the question at the next sitting.

"Whatever communications were made to me, were of a confidential character, and therefore I cannot give any information or particulars," the Attorney-General replied to Kater the next day. "I must therefore courteously decline to answer the second part of the question."[5]

Want's non-answer only fuelled the rumours of a Dean confession, stimulating the newspapers. Premier Reid denied any knowledge of a confession, and reporters then sought out George on the *Wallaby*.

"I haven't the least idea how the story of the confession originated," George told the *Sunday Times*. "I have never discussed the case in any way, and don't intend to, and I think it is very cruel of my enemies to set such a story about, for I can attribute it to no one but those who have tried to do me an injury. Surely I have suffered enough already, and been put to quite enough worry, without having the whole thing revived just when I was expecting to settle down in something like peace and quietness."

"You never made use of any remark that you know of which might be manipulated to spread such a story abroad?" the *Times* reporter asked.

"No, none whatever."[6]

And this was true. Since his release from gaol, George had been very circumspect in what he said about the case to anyone, including close friends.

George was approached by members of the Dean Defence Committee, who convinced him to petition Parliament to seek the source of the rumour. They wrote the petition, due to his weak literacy skills, and George duly signed it. The petition was presented to the House of Assembly on Tuesday, September 24. After outlining the Dean case and repeating

Kater's question, the petition stated: "Your petitioner, therefore, humbly prays that he may be furnished with such particulars as to the author of such statement and the evidence upon which it was made as will enable your petitioner to clear his character from the undeserved stigma which such a statement by a Minister of the Crown has cast upon him."[7]

The next day, Attorney-General Want addressed the Legislative Council after Dean's petition had also been presented there: "[Kater's] question placed me in a very awkward position. If I had stated what had been told to me I should have been guilty of a breach of confidence that had been reposed in me. On the other hand, if I had refused to answer the question it would have left the matter in such a way that everyone would have implied that I had received a confession of Dean's guilt ... Since then the circumstances have changed by a petition presented [by Dean] ... asking for that information. Under these circumstances, I have ascertained from the gentleman, who made the communication to me, that he feels himself relieved from any pledge [of silence on the issue]."[8]

"I have asked my informant to place the whole thing verbatim in writing," Want concluded, "and tomorrow afternoon I will place that statement upon the table of this House."

The next day, Thursday (September 26), Want revealed his source ... Sir Julian Salomons.

He read Sir Julian's letter to the Council word for word.

In it Salomons declared that Mr Meagher had retained him professionally on July 18, two days after the *Daily Telegraph* published its criticism of Meagher's handling of the Dean trial. Meagher wanted his written opinion as to whether the first paragraph of the article was actionable for defamation. Salomons read the paragraph and immediately declared he could not see how Meagher could possibly recover damages over it – after all, Dean had been found guilty at the trial, but was later found not guilty by the Royal Commission.[9]

"But Dean was in fact guilty," Meagher said, "and I absolutely know it."

"But what do you mean?" Salomons asked.

After Dean was convicted, Meagher said, and while agitating for the Royal Commission, he determined to find out whether or not Dean was innocent. So he used a ruse. He visited Dean in his cell and suddenly told him that the police had found out where he bought the poison.

Meagher said Dean turned very pale and asked: "Where do they say I bought the poison?"

"Oh, I don't know that, they won't state," Meagher lied, "but you had better tell us all about it."

Dean then told him the name of the chemist where he obtained the poison. He used two poisons, arsenic and strychnine to make sure of getting rid of her. Just before he was arrested, he took the remains of his poisons and burnt them in the fireplace – if they had arrested him on the day before they did, they would have found the poisons.

Salomons asked Meagher if the chemist had testified at the trial. Meagher said he appeared at both the committal hearing and the trial. Did the chemist lie under oath? No, Meagher replied, he was never asked if he had sold poison to Dean. Salomons said he checked the court records and found this to be true for one particular chemist.

Meagher again visited Salomons in his chambers two days later, on July 20.

"I pointed out to Mr Meagher, among other matters," Salomons wrote, "the unpleasant and embarrassing position he had placed me in. I informed him that, for my own sake, I had in confidence told a member of the bar what he had stated to me. I implored him, by every solemn consideration I could think of, to let the public know that the wife was wholly innocent, and that Dean, though then at liberty, was wholly guilty. I pressed upon him, in the weightiest manner possible, to consider, apart from the awful injury to his wife, the serious and irreparable harm he was doing to the public confidence in the administration of justice. He expressed his sorrow for the position Mrs Dean was in, as being no doubt thought by nearly everybody guilty of a conspiracy to bring her husband to the scaffold by a false charge. He said she was a simpleton, but was no doubt perfectly innocent, and had told the truth. Mr Meagher volunteered to join in aiding her pecuniarily to relieve her from the extreme poverty she was in. I pointed out to him that her poverty was a small consideration, and that he must in some way let the public know that she had been wrongly accused, and that Dean had been properly found guilty by the jury. I advised him to see if he could not, without injury to himself or Mr Crick, to whom he had immediately, after Mr Crick's speech in the Assembly, communicated Dean's confession, undo the wrong that had been done, and force Dean, who had now a full pardon, to confess his guilt, though as a consequence he might have to leave the country. Mr Meagher thanked me for my advice, and said he would carefully consider it and see me again."

Meagher came some days later and showed Salomons some documents, saying it impossible for him to reveal Dean's confession to the public (presumably meaning it would do great damage to Crick and himself). Salomons asked Meagher to take some days and think it over very carefully, and then to come back and see him. But he never did.

"When I became absolutely certain that Mr. Meagher would do nothing," Salomons' letter concluded, "I communicated the whole matter to the Attorney-General."

At 6:30 pm, an *Australian Star* reporter boarded the *Wallaby* as it was about to cast off at Circular Quay, heading for Mosman. He noted that George Dean was obviously unaware of the afternoon's proceedings in Parliament, as passengers were telling a bewildered captain they did not believe he had confessed to Meagher. At Mosman the reporter showed him the just-printed edition of the *Star* and read out Salomons' statements.

"Good God, what lies!" George exclaimed as he heard Meagher's statement of a confession. "I am satisfied I am innocent. They can do what they like."[10]

"Did you ever say anything, to anybody, about poisons?" the reporter asked.

"No, I never did. How could I?"

"Not even to Mr. Meagher?"

"No, nor to anybody."

"Did Mr Meagher ever ask you?"

"Yes, and I always told him that I knew nothing of it."

"How often did Mr Meagher himself visit you in gaol?"

"Once before the trial, once in the condemned cell, and about six times afterwards."

"And there is no foundation for the statement?"

"Not the least. It's a lot of lies."

The statements made in Parliament, the *Star's* report concluded, had not shaken the confidence of the ferry boat captains of Dean's innocence.

A Bruised Ego

The *Star* interviewed Mrs Dean and her mother and found them "highly pleased" with the latest developments. He must be guilty, Mary said, for I am innocent.

Dick Meagher told reporters he would not make any statements just yet, but would soon speak on the issue in Parliament; he was currently discussing it with the Leader of the Opposition.

On learning of developments in Parliament, Paddy Crick rushed back from Maitland. Arriving about 7:30 pm, he read Salomons' letter in a newspaper before addressing the House of Assembly. He had met Sir Julian in the refreshment room after reading the newspaper, Crick declared to the House, and, upset, had used language to him which he now deeply regretted. But what Salomons claimed was completely untrue.

"[Salomons] had stated that I knew, at the time and during the progress of the agitation [for the Royal Commission], that [while] I stood in this House and said that Dean was innocent, that [I knew all along] he was guilty," Crick said passionately. "I said it was untrue, and the man who uttered it [Salomons] was untruthful."

Crick wanted to know why Salomons had not approached him about the issue. Salomons' chambers were next door to his law office, and they practically bumped into each other every day. Salomons claimed he learned of this two months ago, yet not once had Salomons walked next door to speak to him about it, nor had he spoken about it on one of their daily meetings. Salomons was bringing this forward now to deflect attention from Windeyer, who was in trouble again (the Butler-Johnson case).

"It is a somewhat marvellous circumstance that for over two months this wily Jew has kept this sleeping in his bosom," Crick declared, "and that it only finds light when there is a motion on the business-paper against a judge [Windeyer]. He does not dare to say, he does not attempt to say that during these two months, although he states that he is next door to me when he is in his office, he never said a word to me. I am the senior member of the firm. I was the man who moved for the royal commission. I was in Parliament at the time. Why did he not speak to me if he has told the truth?"

If Salomons had taken a retainer from Meagher about the *Daily Telegraph*, Crick continued, why did he then take a retainer from Premier Reid when Meagher and himself issued a writ against the Premier, who used the words of the *Daily Telegraph*?

Crick also attacked Attorney-General Want.

On Friday morning (September 27), members of the Dean Defence Committee again approached George and he gave them an absolute denial of ever making a confession of guilt to Meagher. On their request, he agreed to make a sworn deposition to this effect and, as with the petition, they assisted him to write it, before taking him to Magistrate Sydney Austin for George to sign in his presence.

George's affidavit contained two main statements:

1. I have read the statement made in the Legislative Council last evening (Thursday), as reported in this morning's newspapers, and I absolutely deny that I have ever during my incarceration in Darlinghurst Gaol, or at any other time, made any confession whatsoever as an admission of my guilt, or which might in any way be taken as an admission of guilt, in the case in which I was charged with having administered poison to Mary Dean with intent to kill.

2. I have always asserted, and now most emphatically repeat, that I am absolutely innocent of the said charge; and the statement made as to my admission of purchasing,

obtaining, or procuring from any person whatsoever either strychnine, arsenic, or other poisons is absolutely untrue. I further state that I never handled poison in my life. I make this solemn declaration of the matters aforesaid according to law, and subject to any punishment the law provides for any wilfully false statement in such declaration.

Salomons did not name the chemist from whom Dean was supposed to have obtained poison, but the *Sunday Times* soon worked out that Richard Smith was the only chemist not asked if he had supplied poison to Dean.

"It is true I was not asked," Smith told the *Times*. "If I had, the answer would have been the same as now – that, to the best of my knowledge, I never sold arsenic or strychnine to George Dean."[11]

On Monday morning (September 30), an *Australian Star* reporter again interviewed George: "Why Dean should be dragged back again before the public gaze and criticism, he fails to see, as he has done nothing to merit it. From morning until night, people go down to the ferry to gaze and stare at him, while others take trips to and fro, and the man's life is a continual worry to him on that account."

The *Star* also returned to Mary and her mother: "They are in destitute circumstances, and have to pay a weekly rent of [12] shillings. Their house is a model of neat arrangement of their little stock of household goods, and everything is exceptionally clean."[12]

"While he was in gaol [awaiting trial]," Mary said, "he wrote me very loving letters. He never wrote such loving letters before. I do not think he could have written them by himself."

"Oh! Mother, don't go on like that," Mary said, as her mother's weeping increased.

"I can't help it," Mrs. Seymour sobbed. "My heart and hers

are nearly broken. To think it should be said I tried to poison her! When I was in Oxford Street the other day, people cried out 'Poisoner' to me."

That night, at a banquet held in his honour at the Blayney Town Hall, Paddy Crick stated that over the last six years his firm had been involved in all the major criminal cases in Sydney, but he had only brought the cases of two men before parliament – Ernst Büttner and George Dean – because he had fully believed in the innocence of both those men. Dean had no money, so his case was not pursued for monetary reasons, only a belief in his innocence. Sir Julian Salomons, on the other hand, only ever believed in Dean's guilt. Sir Julian had asked him why he did not act as a counsel in the Dean Royal Commission. He replied that he wanted Sir William Windeyer put in the box so he could question him before the Commissioners, but they refused to allow it, so he stepped aside.[13]

The *Evening News* asked Richard Price, the Member for Gloucester, how his motion before the House (to have Windeyer removed from the bench of the Supreme Court) would be affected if Dean did confess. Price replied that it would be unaffected, he wanted "to be able to look with reverence and homage on the occupants of the bench".[14]

On Tuesday (October 1), Dick Meagher rose to address the House of Assembly (and the overcrowded gallery) to make a "personal explanation", and to call Sir Julian a liar.[15]

"The remarks I make will be in a calm, thoughtful spirit," Meagher said. "Anything I have to say in regard to Sir Julian Salomons will be temperate, and I wish it to be understood that it will be said more in sorrow and pity than in anger."

"As to the alleged confession of George Dean," Meagher

continued, "allow me straight away to state, in order that there may be not the slightest misapprehension, that George Dean never in his life made any confession to me; secondly, that I never in my life made any confession to Sir Julian Salomons ... yet it has remained for me at this hour of the day, as possessor of a terrible secret, to go to Sir Julian Salomons, into the enemy's camp, and to reveal that secret to him, without motive and without gain! ... There has been no motive which could impel me to take such a course in the case from start to finish. I think the whole amount we have received in the case has been some £15. Believing, as I do, in the man's innocence, the butt of my cheque book will show that I have spent over £20 out of my own pocket in agitation [for the Royal Commission]".

Meagher then attacked the Attorney-General.

"Mr. Want is a man who, in connection with the Dean case, went to Darlinghurst and shrieked for Dean's blood, and for the time being he got it. Mr Want is a man – my chambers are adjoining those of Sir Julian Salomons – who is in daily communication with Sir Julian Salomons. This is a matter of notoriety to members of the Dean Defence Committee, some of whom I see now ... Day after day, when I would be going in my office and out of my office – in fact, I think, just preceding the Dean Commission – the Attorney-General fairly well lived at Sir Julian Salomons' chambers."

Meagher read out a lengthy signed document in which he admitted visiting Sir Julian on July [16]. He had asked Mr Pilcher QC for a legal opinion on the paragraph in the *Daily Telegraph*, but he had been too busy to look at it.

He then sought an opinion from Sir Julian: "[Salomons] read the paragraph, and said, 'I think it is actionable, but I am not so sure about the measure of damages you would get. Leave it here, and I will look into it.' I said, 'I wish you would give me an opinion as early as possible.' As I was rising to go he said, 'Well, how is Dean getting on?' This was the first time I had spoken to Sir Julian since the royal commission. I replied, 'I have not seen him for some time.' He then said, 'Ah, he's an arch-scoundrel, that fellow. He was fortunate in getting off before the commission.' I said, 'Don't you think an innocent man is entitled to get off?' He replied, 'You know about his innocence as well as I do'; and in an excited way said, 'Why, if all the angels from heaven came down and swore he was innocent, I would not believe them.' I replied, 'Oh, Sir Julian, you are prejudiced against the man'."

Sir Julian complained that the Weyntons should have been put on trial as they supplied Dean with strychnine. He told Salomons he was positive that they had "no connection" with the Dean case.

Meagher continued: "I said, 'Could he not get it from a chemist?' He then in a most solemn manner said, 'That is the very matter I want to see you about.' He said to me slowly, 'Do you remember the case in the police court?' I said, 'Yes.' He said, 'Do you remember asking all the chemists but one a certain question?' I said I could not remember, and I did not know what he was referring to. Then, opening a drawer in his desk, he said, 'Since the commission closed, I have noticed this matter; it has worried me very much, and you are the only living soul I have spoken to about it.' He then put on the desk the printed depositions of the police court (which honourable members have seen laid on the table of this House), and they were turned back on a certain page as if they had been recently referred to. He then called my attention to the fact that Smith, the chemist, was not asked about selling poison at the police court, and I replied, 'Well,

A Bruised Ego

I really thought I asked them all, and I then said, 'but I attach no importance to that.' He then said, in a most earnest manner, 'My dear Meagher, did you not omit to ask that very question because he was the man who sold Dean poison?' I said, 'Certainly not. I never had the least motive in not asking him the question; besides, I fancy Dean had less transactions with Smith than any of them'."

Meagher told Salomons he had to leave: "He then, in shaking hands, held my hand, and, looking me in the face fixedly, said, 'Look here, Meagher, you hold the solution of this terrible case, and, if I were in your position, I could not rest till I told the truth.' I replied, 'I have no secret, and if I had it would remain in me'."

Meagher said he fully believed in George Dean's innocence and that Sir Julian was the "creature of a mental, uncontrollable impulse" – he was hallucinating.

As Meagher sat down, he was loudly cheered.

On the next afternoon (October 2), Sir Julian Salomons addressed the Legislative Council, reaffirming the contents of his letter previously read to the Council. He named Richard Smith as the chemist who supplied Dean with poison; in court, Meagher asked three of four chemists if they supplied poison to Dean, but he did not ask Smith. And after Dean was convicted, Crick and Meagher "conspired" to bring about a royal commission. Crick was just as deeply involved in this "conspiracy" as Meagher.[16]

"There is not a man in the country who can truthfully say that I have ever shown the slightest sign of any hallucination at all – except one," Sir Julian said, indicating Meagher. "I have done nothing which will bring shame into my face or force me to draw back one inch from the accusation that, in the name of eternal justice, I launch against Crick, against Meagher, and against Dean."

Sir Julian Salomons, left, and the *Bulletin's* take on Want's reaction to Salomons' revelation.

He told Meagher that he had been placed in a terrible situation by him: "You have disclosed to me that you and your partner, knowing that the man who was found guilty was rightly found guilty, set your wits to work to create an agitation in the public mind and in the press, leading to the conviction [belief] that an innocent man had been brought to the edge of the scaffold. And not only that, but you have left, and are now leaving, that unfortunate woman, who is only somewhere about 21 years of age, the wife of this man, under the charge of being worse than a murderess against her own husband ... I cannot let you leave things as they are. You must in some way, though it may be a bitter draught for you to swallow, let this country know that Dean ought to have died on the scaffold, and that the wife has done nothing in the matter that was criminal."

There ensued a lengthy to and fro between Salomons and Charles Pilcher, formerly the opposing counsel at the Dean

Royal Commission. Pilcher said that justice had demanded the Dean Royal Commission and, unlike Sir Julian, he had kept his conclusions about it to himself.[17]

"I have expressed no opinion whatsoever about that trial!" Sir Julian exclaimed.

"My honourable and learned friend has expressed over and over again his conviction of Dean's guilt," Pilcher said.

"I have only stated what I told Mr. Meagher. I have never gone into that question!"

"I think the honourable and learned member has forgotten that over and over again he reiterated his conviction of Dean's guilt."

"Certainty, I have always stated he was guilty, and I believe it still; but I have not gone into the matter of the commission!"

"After careful consideration of the evidence taken before the commission, I had the strongest conviction, which is not shaken one iota now – and that is quite apart from the question whether Mr Meagher made the assertion to Sir Julian Salomons or not – that Dean was not guilty," Pilcher said. "And had it not been that Sir Julian Salomons has said over and over again what his conviction is, I would not have said anything about it … [Sir Julian] proposed to me that we should meet in consultation with Mr Meagher for the purpose deliberately of entrapping him into a statement."

"I never said so!" Salomons exclaimed. "I said the intention in my mind was to obtain a witness to what he said!"

For him to meet with Sir Julian and Mr Meagher in this manner, Pilcher said, was to go behind Dean's back, building up a case of his guilt. To do this, after being Dean's counsel, would justify his disrobement as a barrister. He wrote to Sir Julian to say that if such a meeting did take place, it would have to be "sacred and secret" – nothing could be revealed to anyone about it. Pilcher maintained that the confidentiality of his clients was paramount.

Pilcher contacted William Goddard, on the Dean Defence Committee, and told him in confidence of Salomons' claims. Goddard sought a statement from Meagher and received in return: "I did have an interview with Sir Julian Salomons, and I may have made a jocular observation when he was speaking of Dean's guilt; but I never told him that Dean had ever made a confession of his guilt to me." The Defence Committee sought and obtained assurances from Dean and, later, the petition to parliament and the sworn statement.

Three days later, at midday on Saturday (October 5), Dick Meagher was arrested and taken to the No 1 Police Station in Clarence Street. Paddy Crick learned of Meagher's arrest while lunching at an Oyster Bar in King Street, previous to attending the afternoon Rose Hill races where he had horses running. He immediately caught a cab to the police station to bail Meagher out. On arrival, he too was arrested. Both were taken to the Central Police Station.[18]

George Dean made his last run of the day on the *Wallaby*, and as he stepped off the *Wallaby* at Circular Quay, police arrested him.

The charge against all three: *conspiracy to pervert the course of justice*.

Appearing before Stipendiary Magistrate Smithers, Meagher and Crick were represented by solicitor Robert Levien, the Member for Quirindi, who had been lunching with Crick. The Crown strongly opposed bail but both men were released mid-afternoon on a bail of £1,500 each. Later, George Dean, still in his ferry-captain's uniform, was also bailed for £1,500 – for him an enormous sum – with three men going £500

A Bruised Ego

A newspaper depiction of George's arrest on the *Wallaby*.

surety each for him, including his best friend Harry Paul.

The sensational arrests came out of the blue, catching all by surprise. The arrested three were not given the grounds for their arrest, and were left bemused. The next day, Sunday, *Truth* reported its catalyst: *on Friday, chemist Richard Smith had confessed to supplying Dean with poison.*[19]

Out on bail, George stoically continued his duties on the *Wallaby* despite the reporters and a multitude of gawking onlookers. The ferry was constantly full of passengers for the twenty-minute ride across the harbour, and hundreds of men, women and children continually crowded around the wharves at Mosman and Circular Quay to catch a glimpse of him. Despite the chemist's confession, the Dean Defence Committee and other friends still expressed their belief in his innocence. As George performed his normal duties, including helping little children down the gangplank, Harry Paul and another friend were at his side to ward off any awkward situations.

While awaiting bail after his arrest, Paddy Crick had promised reporters to attack Attorney-General Want at the next sitting of the Legislative Assembly, but on the following Tuesday (October 8) the packed House and crowded gallery received instead a very subdued and contrite "personal explanation" from him.

Crick said he had not been involved in Dean's trial, Dick Meagher had handled that. Up until the night of Dean's release under pardon, he had only seen Dean on one occasion – that was the day his trial started. In the days following Dean's conviction, he read in the newspapers the criticism of the trial conduct of the judge, Sir William Windeyer.[20]

"I then asked my partner," Crick said, "what was his candid opinion as to his [Dean's] guilt or innocence. He then told me that he was convinced that the man was an absolutely innocent man. I had great reliance in his judgment; but being, nevertheless, peculiarly cautious before I would take a grave public step, I determined to satisfy myself that in my own judgment I should be justified in using my position here in Parliament to reopen such a very grave and serious charge. Let me say in passing, in regard to a taunt sometimes hurled at me, that since the case of Büttner I have not used my public position to reopen a trial. ... I then asked Meagher what made him entertain the conviction that Dean was an innocent man, and he told me of the episode of the detective, which has already been mentioned, telling him that he had been some weeks before with a view to arrest Dean on this very charge of attempting to poison his wife; and of the wife and mother-in-law stating at the trial that they afterwards took the chops and tea alleged to be poisoned.

"I asked Meagher what corroboration he had ... He told

A Bruised Ego

A satirical cartoon by the *Bulletin* shows Dean whispering into Meagher's ear, who whispers into Salomons' ear, who whispers into Want's ear, who trumpets it to all and sundry. At the same time Justice Windeyer is doing a "demonic dance" and singing "I told you so".

me that certainly one and perhaps two reporters could bear him out. I sent for one of these reporters … [who] bore out in every detail what Meagher had told me … I said to Meagher [before Dean was reprieved] … 'Go up to Darlinghurst and see him, Dick, and tell him … that as matters stand, in view of the recommendation of the jury, he will certainly be reprieved, and will not go to the scaffold; tell him, and say it is a certainty, he will be reprieved, and that with time on his side … he may be again a free man ... on the other hand, tell him that if I go in and get from the Government a commission to reopen this case, it will be reopened on all sides, and the Government will use every effort in their power, exhaust every resource, to see if he ever bought poison; and if they find out he ever bought poison, tell him he will hang, as sure as God made little apples'.

"My partner came back to me … and said, 'He told me to tell

you to go on; he had nothing to fear; he never bought poison, or handled it, and he defied the Government and all the police force to prove that he ever handled poison in his life'.

"Now, I appeal to honourable members if that was not a sufficiently cautious preparation to justify a man in asking this House and the Government to reopen the case. And on that I went on."

Crick said he pursued the establishment of the Royal Commission, but did not take part in it, not because he doubted Dean's innocence, but because Pilcher declined to take the course he wanted – to put Windeyer before the Commission and question him.

While he was campaigning for the election he heard a number of rumours of a Dean confession. But the one that really concerned him was of Meagher telling Salomons Dean had confessed.

"I asked Mr Meagher, 'Did you ever make such a statement?' And my words, sir, were sadly prophetic – sadly prophetic. He assured me that he had not given Sir Julian any reason or said anything to him that would justify him in saying that Dean had admitted to him his guilt of attempt to murder. I said, 'I am glad to hear it, Dick, because if you did and it comes out, it will kill you, as sure as you stand before me.' I heard no more of that matter until I saw the public proceedings connected with it. I was at East Maitland ... Mr Meagher did admit then that he had a conversation with Sir Julian; but he did not admit that he had said anything that would justify Sir Julian in saying that Dean had made a confession ... that he had been 'pulling Sir Julian's leg'."

After listening to Sir Julian Salomons' speech in its entirety, Crick said, his belief in Meagher was shaken. He was told that

Meagher's denial of Salomons in the House was "the voice of Meagher but the mind of Crick" – and this was to vastly underrate Meagher's ability. He apologised profusely for his attacks on Sir Julian.

Even after his arrest, he was not really concerned about the truth of Meagher's statements. The next day, Sunday, Meagher reiterated to him his denial of Salomons. But he thought there was which was tearing at Meagher's heart, something that Meagher felt he should tell him, but could not. At that point, Crick said, he began to believe in Dean's guilt.

Crick spoke to Meagher on Monday: "I pointed out to him that if there was guilt he was dragging into that guilt one who had been his true and best friend from boyhood up, and who he knew in his heart had no hand, act, or part, or knowledge of this matter. Yesterday evening he told he had a terrible secret to impart. Then I said, 'I knew it, my judgment has not been at fault'; but I added, 'Dick, let us have somebody over here now to hear what this is, because you are in deep water'. A certain person came in; he heard what was said – he heard it all – and I then implored Mr Meagher that he should do what was right and take the path of duty, which was the path of truth. I could not move him."

This morning he was still unable to change Meagher's mind. So he sent for Alice Meagher, his wife, to listen to what had happened and for Meagher to be advised by her.

The result was a sworn deposition signed by Richard Denis Meagher, which Paddy Crick read to the House:

"I am determined to endure mental torture no longer, nor to stifle the voice of truth.

"Being of the opinion that Dean was not guilty, and that his trial was an unfair one, I decided to use my utmost endeavours to secure his release. I became aware after his conviction, while in the condemned cell, of his guilt; and coming from Darlinghurst in the tram I was torn asunder as to whether I should upset the verdict or let things remain as they were.

"I knew the man who had been my best friend in life, Mr Crick, would never aid in Parliament or otherwise a movement for the reopening of the case if he knew Dean was guilty. I concealed the terrible fact from him and everyone else, including Mr Pilcher and the members of the [Dean] Defence Committee, and as there is a 'destiny which shapes our ends, rough hew them how we will',* Sir Julian Salomons did become from me the repository of the secret which is substantially given by him in his statement read in the legislative Council.

"I regret that he did my partner an injustice in referring to his knowledge of the matter. I did some time after Dean's release, and after I had spoken to Sir Julian Salomons, deny to Mr Crick that there was any foundation for rumours he referred to in connection with an alleged confession, and it was only yesterday I made to him a full confession, which I now in pain and sorrow make to the public. I have contradicted Sir Julian Salomons in the Legislative Assembly, as I deluded myself that in loyalty to Dean on a breach of confidence I was justified in fighting with any weapons. When I found my error of judgment has forced me into falsehood to cover up my indiscretion and to shield Dean I was prepared for the sacrifice; but when I found that my action was to engulf innocent people and place them in a felon's dock, as I see by the papers this morning other 'prominent men to be arrested', I determined that unless I extricated the innocent I would

---

* Hamlet, Act V, Scene 2

A Bruised Ego

A newspaper depiction of Meagher's consultation with Salomons. As a client of Salomons, Meagher expected complete client confidentiality. At the same time, ego did not allow him to respect the confidentiality of his own client.

be guilty of flagrant moral cowardice. And although I have committed a great error of judgment, which, in its terrible consequences, has almost unhinged my intellect and brought dire tribulation on those dear to me, I still have a sense of justice, and only wish I could put back the universe again to the day I made my first error. I find, in view of the arrest of an innocent person, I can no longer keep this terrible silence ..."

Meagher went on to resign from Parliament and to say he was still young, not yet thirty, and would continue his life "in some other portion of the globe".

Detective Alexander Hinds, in charge of the conspiracy case, had been forewarned of a possible confession by Crick in Parliament. He went to a Water Police Magistrate and, obtaining a warrant for the arrest of George Dean, gave it to Detective Jones, who then boarded the crowded *Wallaby* at Circular Quay and rode back and forth to Mosman, keeping

George under observation. Hinds was concerned that if a confession did eventuate, and Dean heard of it, he might make a run for it or even commit suicide.[21]

Hinds sat behind the Speaker listening intently to Crick's speech. As Crick read out the first words of Meagher's sworn confession, he quietly left and sent a message to Jones to make the arrest. At four o'clock, Jones allowed George to put out the gangplank at Circular Quay, and for most passengers to go ashore, before taking him into custody. George, who had no idea of his imminent arrest, sent for Captain Summerbell to find a replacement for him. Taken before the Water Police Court, George was charged with perjury and remanded without bail.

As George was being transferred to Darlinghurst Gaol, a policeman, as directed by Hinds, gave him a copy of a newspaper containing Meagher's confession so he could record his reaction.

"I don't know, I am sure," Dean said after reading it. "It looks as though they were trying to save themselves and letting me go."

The next morning (Wednesday, October 9), George appeared before Magistrate James Giles (who had conducted his committal hearing at North Sydney) charged with making a false declaration – his recent petition to the Government claiming innocence, written by the Dean Defence Committee, and signed by him in the presence of a magistrate. He was remanded in custody.

Later in the day, William Goddard and Robert Moodie of the Dean Defence Committee visited George at Darlinghurst after obtaining official permission. As George was brought into a room at the gaol complex, they noted the great change in his countenance – he appeared greatly depressed, his face was pale and he was sweating profusely – they had never seen him like this, even after he was convicted at his trial.

Moodie told George that it was possible that a fresh charge of attempted murder would be laid against him.

"I must say this to you," Moodie said, "that the men who, in your trouble, have worked for you, worked as neither you nor any other man could have expected. This morning Mr Goddard and I became – for the first time – impressed with your guilt, and now, Dean, are you really guilty? Take time and consider before you answer. If you are really guilty say so as you would before your Maker."[22]

"Mr Goddard and Mr Moodie, I'm guilty," George said.

"I implicitly trusted Mr Meagher and followed his directions," George said. "I admitted my guilt to Mr Meagher in the corridor near the condemned cell, and Mr Meagher urged upon me the necessity of keeping it secret at the same time promising to do so himself."

"Where did you get the poison?" Goddard asked.

"I bought it from Smith the chemist," George replied.

"Were you on friendly terms with Smith?"

"No, but I bought it from him."

"What did you buy?"

"Both arsenic and strychnine."

"What did you do with it?"

"I mixed some of it in the lemon syrup."

"Did you burn the rest of it?"

"No."

George denied ever putting poison in the tea or the porter, just the lemon syrup.

Moodie wrote out a confession and the two men, together with Governor Herbert, witnessed George signing the confession: "I, George Dean, charged and on remand, hereby state willingly and without any pressure whatsoever from outside or any source, that I am guilty of the charge of perjury. I declare I purchased both arsenic and strychnine from Mr Smith, chemist, West Street, North Sydney, and that I have all through denied my guilt at the instigation of Mr Meagher, my solicitor. And I further state I did confess my guiltiness to Meagher in the corridor of the condemned cell at Darlinghurst. I also state that no other person but Meagher and Mr Green, clerk to Messrs Crick and Meagher clerk, knew of my confession."

All were concerned at the level of George's despondency, so much so that a hammock, requested by George, was withdrawn in case it was used as a means to suicide.

In the afternoon, George appeared before Magistrate Johnson at the Water Police Court, charged with perjury. The sworn affidavit signed by him on September 27 was read out. The Magistrate asked George, without legal counsel, how he pleaded.

"Guilty," said George.

During the sittings of the Dean Royal Commission, the newsboys, selling newspapers on Sydney's street corners, would call out "George Innocent Dean". Now, the *Australian Star* noted, they were calling out "George Guilty Dean".[23]

Here, finally, was an *undeniable* answer to the question of who poisoned Mary Dean.

And without Dick Meagher's bruised ego, the question may never have been answered.

10.

Perjury

> "Why, I don't exactly know about perjury, my dear sir,"
> replied the little gentleman.
> "Harsh word, my dear sir, very harsh word indeed.
> It's a legal fiction, my dear sir, nothing more."
> **The Pickwick Papers by Charles Dickens**

The Australian public was more than stunned at the sudden revelation of George's guilt. Initial disbelief was followed by enormous feelings of betrayal – they had believed so fervently in George's apparent high character, in his claims of innocence – especially the Dean Defence Committee, who had spoken with him personally so often, accepting his many assurances of innocence and working so hard to free him. There were mutterings that he must be insane, while others declared him to be a simpleton. All of which denied the logic that, in the first place, few men would not lie to avoid being hanged, and then continue the lie to escape a life sentence in gaol.

Even following George's arrest, Captain Summerbell had declared to reporters that he still retained a belief in George's innocence. After George's confession, the *Daily Telegraph* reported the Captain as "prostrated".

"I once travelled to Mosman Bay with Dean," Captain Summerbell told the reporter, "and I was really astonished to see the respectable class of people who spoke to him, and the deep regard they seemed to have for him. Dean assured me over and over again of his innocence, and when he was taken away by the detectives on Tuesday evening, I had every hope and belief that he would soon be at liberty to resume his work … I never thought he was deceiving me, and now, when I think of what has passed, I feel unable to speak."[1]

For Fred Konnecke Snr, whom George called "Dad", George's confession cut deeper still.

"I have stuck to him all through, and always thought he was innocent," he told the *Sydney Morning Herald*. "Had I believed otherwise, I would have cut him down with a cleaver myself. And Mrs Konnecke stuck up for him through thick and thin. But I am glad he did not tell me of his guilt. Even today out at Glebe Island among the butchers, I took his part, believing that he was an injured man … I always thought so much of him. I have a half-brother [William Finch] of his here with me now; he has been very broken down about the whole affair, and says that he could shoot Dean now himself. As for me, I never thought he would have poisoned a cat, let alone his own wife."[2]

"Will you see him at the court tomorrow?" the *Herald* asked.

"No. I do not want to see him anymore," Konnecke replied. "We had arranged to send all his meals on to the Court, but no meals now. I am done with him. I never have been so taken down in my life as I have been this time … I am really sorry for Mrs Dean now as things have turned out. It was terrible for an innocent woman to be hooted as she was at the police court."

The *Daily Telegraph* interviewed Mary Dean and her mother, who was nursing Florence, describing Mary as "dignified and refined".[3]

"It has been terrible!" said Caroline. "What I have gone through has been dreadful!"

Why did Dean poisoned her?

Perjury

"That is what we always wondered," Caroline said.

Was he very fond of you?

"Well, he must have been, or he would not have poisoned me," Mary replied sardonically.

Had she had many rows with Dean?

"No, not many," Mary replied. "But he would pick a quarrel out of nothing."

The interview was interrupted by Detective Keating, who lived nearby, dropping in to give Mary a copy of a newspaper containing Dean's written confession.

"You know that he's confessed that he gave you the poison himself?" Keating asked.

"No, I didn't," Mary replied. "I had heard something about it. That was all."

In point of fact, the reporter noted, the unfortunate woman had grown so accustomed to hearing that she had poisoned herself that she took some convincing that someone else had actually poisoned her.

Keating read out the confession to Mary.

If she had her way, Mary said, George would never have been charged with poisoning her.

"The police brought the charge," Mary said, "and we have had to suffer for it."

Mary stated that whenever she appeared in public, she had been abused and, as a consequence, she had been kept a virtual prisoner inside her house.

"A few people stood by us, it is true," Mary said, "but they were very few."

They were interrupted again by a man offering to take up a collection to help Mary and her mother get out of their financial difficulties. He took their silence as acquiescence and left.

Earlier this afternoon, Mary said, a man driving a cart – a working man – had pulled up outside their house and pushed a few coins under her door.

Justice Sir William Windeyer continually refused to answer any questions about George's confession from reporters, but let his guard down completely at a dinner involving a number of clergymen at Government House, Adelaide. The *Evening News* reported that the Judge found himself "in sympathetic company" as Rev Fitchett, for one, commented that Sir William had been so "abused and vilified" but had now been shown "to be in the right".[4]

The *Evening News* report continued: "When the time came for him to respond, he completely broke down. For weeks past, he said, his back had been against the wall; the current of public feeling had been adverse to him; and he had been represented as unjust and cruel. But through it all he had been sustained by a consciousness of his own integrity. Now that the reaction had set in, the kind expressions, which poured in upon him, were more than he could well bear. The judge's utterance was choked with sobs, and there was not one present but was deeply moved. 'The stern and cruel judge' of popular estimation was after all shown to be a man of deep and tender feeling."

On Thursday afternoon (October 10), George – still wearing the ferry captain's uniform in which he was arrested – appeared at Central Police Court before Magistrate William Johnson for a committal hearing. Newspapers reported that thousands had tried to get into the court. With an over-packed courtroom, officials had been forced to lock all the doors, even the windows. Barrister Charles Wade conducted the prosecution. Many Members of Parliament were in attendance, including Paddy Crick and his

Perjury

A newspaper sketch of the crowd outside Central Criminal Court, unable to get in.

counsel Robert Levien, but George had no counsel representing him. On several occasions during the hearing, at the mention of Meagher's name, Levien interjected and exchanged words with Wade – clearly Crick and Levien were there to look after the interests of Crick and Meagher, not George Dean.

The charge of wilfully signing a false document on September 27 was read out and, unaware he was not required to say anything, George said, "Guilty."

Henry Austin JP confirmed that he had witnessed George signing the document. William Goddard gave evidence of Dean's recent confession to the Dean Defence Committee.

Although he could not remember the date, chemist Richard Smith declared that George had approached him in his shop for arsenic to use on a bicycle tyre.

"As I gave it to him," Smith declared, "I said I need not put it in my books. To the best of my knowledge I did not charge him for it."[5]

Smith was quibbling here, trying to claim he had not really

Richard Smith. His chemist shop was in West Street, North Sydney.

lied to the police when they had originally canvassed the North Shore chemists and he denied selling arsenic to George – as he had *given* it to him gratis, he had not actually *sold* it to him. Obviously Smith was trying to avoid the repercussions of illegally selling arsenic.

Since then, Smith continued, Dean had been in his shop once, about a week before his first arrest. He next saw Dean on August 1, while catching the 11:30 ferry after attending the theatre. He complained to Dean about sending Daniel Green, who (he believed) worked for Crick and Meagher, to tell him about his confession to Meagher.

"I was angry and remonstrated with him," Smith deposed, "and Dean said that he had confessed to Mr Meagher that he had bought the poison from me. I replied, 'You should not have told him that, because I did not sell you poison.' ... Dean was cursing and swearing all the way over in the boat. I told him I did not sell him poison, but I gave it to him. He said, 'Don't you remember me having a conversation with you one day in your shop about getting same arsenic to fix cement for an india-rubber tyre? The first lot you gave me I accidentally threw it behind the fire and burnt it. I had a second lot off you.'

… I have a recollection about the second lot that Dean came into the shop when I was alone. It was about a fortnight after the first occasion. I can't remember the date. He was afraid my assistant [in the shop] would let it out … I said, 'He is so sleepy-headed I don't suppose he knows anything about it.' I asked Dean on the boat if he sent Crick and Meagher's clerk [Daniel Green] to me, and he said, 'Yes.' I asked him the meaning of it. I said, 'This young man came to put me on my guard, that the Government was likely to offer me a good reward to 'split' and say I sold Dean poison.' I told the clerk and Dean I was not to be bought and sold like that. I was angry, but Dean did not seem to be angry. He took it as a matter of course. I said, 'I will not say anything about it.' Dean said, 'Did you not notice you were never asked [in court] if you sold me poison?' The clerk [also] told me that. All I said to that was that I should say nothing about it unless I was put on my oath. That was the last time I saw Dean. I have no doubt Dean had the arsenic off me."

"Did you give him strychnine?" Prosecutor Wade asked.

"No, sir," Smith replied. "I don't think to the best of my belief be had strychnine off me. I admit the arsenic."

This was a rather weak denial; the source of the strychnine was never established in court, but in all probability it also came from Smith.

Magistrate Johnson asked George if he had any questions for Smith. George was only keen to assert he had *paid* for the poison.

"In reference to the conversation on the boat, did you not say you made a point of seeing me that night?"

"Yes."

"Did you not say to me to swear you never sold me the poison?"

"I did not."

Justice on Trial

"Did you not say, if it comes out I should say you gave it to me?"

"No, I did not. I think you once said [to me] I should say you never had poison from me."

"That is all I have to say," George said finally, "I paid you for it."

William Padley, Smith's shop assistant, had little to add on the second day of the hearing.

Magistrate Johnson formally committed George to stand trial.

In the days following the committal hearing, police collected ashes from the chimney in George's former North Shore house and took them to the Government Analyst to check for arsenic. The ashes were soon confirmed to contain arsenic.

The law partnership of Crick and Meagher was dissolved, and the nameplate at the front of the office was replaced with one bearing Crick's name only.

A committee was established to take up a subscription to financially aid Mary and her mother with offices named throughout Sydney to accept money.

Police searched for Daniel Green, who had gone into hiding. A week later he surrendered himself to police. Green was also charged with perverting the course of justice. A second charge of perverting the course of justice was also laid against him, involving an unconnected divorce case. Police opposed bail, unusual for this offence, but he was bailed for the exorbitant amounts of £1,500 and £1,000 respectively on each charge.

The four alleged conspirators – Meagher, Crick, Dean and Green – appeared in Court on October 15, and were remanded. At its conclusion, Robert Levien began speaking to George, but was prevented by a warder. Levien obtained the Magistrate's permission and continued speaking to George, probably suggesting he seek legal representation – it was

Perjury

certainly in Crick and Meagher's interests that he do so.

Mrs Jane Reynolds, the wife of the publican at the Young Australia Hotel in Riley Street, Surry Hills, gave evidence to the Royal Commission of Mary Dean being drunk at her hotel. On October 18, she was charged with perjury in giving this evidence, and was remanded and bailed.

Both George's brother, William Finch, and his "Dad", Fred Konnecke, had recovered from the initial shock of George's confession, and were among the few who were prepared to stand by him. George was not permitted any visitors, but had been able to write letters to them. Henry Cato, who had worked with Dick Meagher to obtain the Royal Commission, was another standing by George. George wrote to William and asked him to take a letter to Cato asking if legal counsel could be provided for him. Fred Konnecke also offered to help as much financially as he could to provide George with legal representation.

George wrote: "... With his [Konnecke's] assistance you may be able to get a strong one [lawyer]. I know now I have been very foolish [to confess and to plead guilty], but I was in a terrible state of mind, and with the extra worry I am broken hearted. I am also very thankful for what you have done, and hope to see you when the authorities permit."[6]

"I am tired at heart of the case," Cato told reporters, "but as I told Dean, though everyone else may desert him, I will stand by him until he is either acquitted or convicted. His bicycle has been handed over to me to dispose of to raise funds to fee counsel ... Anyone desirous of helping the fund can either forward subscriptions to Mr Konnecke, Queen Street, Woollahra, or to myself, Belmore Markets."

On Friday, October 18, it was announced that George had

engaged barrister Colonna Close and solicitor Joseph Gorrick to represent him.[7] They went to Darlinghurst Gaol but were unable to speak with him as he was permitted no visitors – he was being kept in strict isolation, unable to speak to anyone and under 24-hour observation, imposed at the request of Attorney-General Want, who feared possible collusion with Crick and Meagher before the trial (letters were permitted as their contents were checked by gaol authorities). Eventually the lawyers were able to get the Attorney-General's permission to speak to their client. Following their visit, and probably a few threats to the Attorney-General of court action, the tight gaol restrictions (basically solitary confinement) on George were lifted – certainly they were dubious for a prisoner still to face trial, but easily imposed on an unrepresented prisoner – and he was then permitted visitors as well as to leave his cell for daily exercise with other prisoners.

The next day he was visited in his cell by sister Jane Finch.[8]

The lawyers declared that George would be pleading not guilty to all charges against him.

When Jane Reynolds arrived at Water Police Court for her committal hearing on the perjury charge, she received a second charge, that of perverting the course of justice, making her the fifth conspirator. She was remanded and bailed at £200.

On the perjury charge, Prosecutor Charles Heydon called his first witness, Detective Hector McLean, the arresting officer. On arresting her, McLean declared, Mrs Reynolds said: "I told the truth. The woman came to my house right enough. I picked her out of 25 others at the hospital." One day a man had shown her three photographs. She picked one of them as the woman who came to her hotel drunk. The man told her

Perjury

Mrs Jane Reynolds of the Young Australia Hotel was charged with perjury in claiming at the Royal Commission that Mary Dean visited her hotel.

it was Mrs Dean. Afterwards a man named Green came to her hotel and showed her a photograph – it was the same woman. She was asked to do it to save an innocent man. She was given nothing to do it. She had then visited the hospital and picked her out.

Rose Kemp, a former barmaid at the Reynolds hotel, remembered a woman coming to the hotel drunk, having arrived in a cab, as described by Mrs Reynolds to the Royal Commission.

"Was this Mrs Dean?" the Prosecutor asked.[9]

"No." replied Kemp.

"Nothing like her?"

"No."

"You're positive of that?"

"Yes."

Kemp said she met Reynolds in the street after she gave evidence to the Royal Commission. Reynolds told her she was positive it was Mrs Dean and that she had visited the offices of Crick and Meagher to tell them so. Crick snubbed her but Meagher said her evidence was worth £50. She had also written to Meagher to see if she could bring an action for slander against Sir Julian Salomons.

Justice on Trial

Defence attorney William Roberts told the Bench it was simply a case of mistaken identity. Magistrate Smithers committed Jane Reynolds to stand trial.

With the trial of George Dean due to begin on Thursday, October 24, a subpoena was sent to Bessie Adey to appear as a witness for George. Her evidence at the Royal Commission had been sensational as she contradicted Mary Dean's assertion that the cup of tea had a bitter taste. Mary had conceded that Bessie sipped the tea and said to her "it tasted all right". Barrister Charles Wade, who was now prosecuting Dean and who would be cross-examining her, had asserted to the Commission that Bessie was lying, stating she had personally told him at the trial, outside the courtroom, that she had put the cup to her lips but did not actually taste it.

Friends said that ever since the Royal Commission, she had aged greatly and her hair had turned white. George's confession had further upset her and she had told one neighbour that it was "worrying her to death". Since receiving the subpoena, she would burst into tears at the thought of giving evidence at the upcoming trial, and was not eating.[10]

Her husband Tom rose, as usual, at 2:30 am on Wednesday morning, the eve of the trial, and Bessie made him a cup of tea. He had to collect the morning newspapers from the Milsons Point wharf before making his morning deliveries. She went into their yard with him and held the horse while Tom attached the cart. At 5:00 am their 22 year-old daughter Ethel rose. Usually Bessie and Ethel both walked some distance to pick up newspapers off Tom to be sold in the shop to early morning customers. On this morning, Ethel suggested her mother go back to bed instead, and brought her a cup of tea before leaving to pick up the papers by herself.

Ethel returned an hour or so later but received no answer from her mother when she knocked on the front door of the shop. She entered the house round the back but did not find her mother in bed, nor could she find her anywhere else in the house. Ethel called out to Phillip Walke, who lived next door, that her mother was missing. He immediately came into the yard and noticed that the covering over an old well had been removed. The 5 metre well contained water to a depth of about 1.5 metres. He took a clothes line prop and poked it into the water to discover Bessie's body. Putting a ladder down the well, Phillip and a neighbour managed to get the body out of the well. Over the next two hours they tried resuscitating Bessie, dressed in her nightgown, but all to no avail.

Tom was contacted and returned home in a very distressed state. On a table in the house, they found an envelope with a message scribbled on it: "Goodbye all. I cannot bear it. Goodbye my darling husband."

The inquest determined her death was caused by drowning.

Tragically, Bessie's suicide was an apparent confirmation that she had lied to the Royal Commission.

The next day, George stood trial before Acting Justice Alfred Backhouse at Central Criminal Court on the charge of making a false declaration. George pleaded not guilty. Colonna Close vainly contended that the Royal Pardon received by George included the charge of making a false declaration.

"It seems to me," Justice Backhouse said, "that he was pardoned for one specific crime."[11]

"Had that crime not been committed," Close replied, "these charges would not have arisen."

Backhouse dismissed the argument, but reserved the point (for a possible challenge to the Supreme Court).

As the trial continued, Henry Austin and Richard Smith gave evidence much as they did at the committal hearing. William Goddard told of George making a written confession; he admitted that George did not look healthy and was certainly agitated at the time but denied he was dazed. George was permitted to make a statement to the jury without cross-examination.

"Those troubles coming up one after another nearly drove me mad," George said, calmly and deliberately. "I was arrested on the Saturday off the boat for conspiracy and I took it to heart. I was bailed out on the Sunday morning, and returned to my work. Hundreds of persons gazed at me, and asked me questions. On the Monday they did the same thing … The detectives were numerous during the two days on the boat. On the Tuesday evening I was again arrested. I saw several friends that I knew and their crying out after me completely took effect on me."

Reporters told him of Meagher saying he had confessed, that Meagher exonerated Crick, and would probably escape punishment other than being struck off as a solicitor. He wanted to punish Meagher. He read the papers and what they said about him, it was very cruel. He could not sleep.

"Next morning," George said, "I was run into the police court, and then I was taken to gaol. When I got to gaol I fairly collapsed – I was broken down, and I did not know what I was doing or saying. I remember Mr. Goddard and Mr Moodie coming there. They told me that the Defence Committee were put into a serious position by what Mr Meagher had said. Hearing that, I broke down because of these people being put to trouble on my account. I have no further recollection of what I said. Whatever I said, I said in vengeance against Mr Meagher. On the Monday night three detectives came into the gaol to see me. No one was allowed to see me; they kept me in a separate cell under observation all the time. They spoke to me of this confession that I had made. It was the first time that I know I had made a confession They tried to call it to my memory, and I remembered a little of it with reference to the committee being placed in a serious position through what Mr Meagher had said ... I have said things at random, not knowing at times what I have been saying."

George denied ever confessing to Meagher. Meagher told him a sworn affidavit had been made by a chemist declaring he sold George poison. He said to Meagher: "It is false – no chemist ever supplied me with poison." Meagher replied: "That is all I want to know."

"I was not in my right senses the morning I made the statement to Mr Goddard," George said in conclusion. "I was so worried with what had happened that I was completely dazed. I have had a good character since I have been working for myself – since I was 8 years of age – and have saved several lives."

In his final address to the jury, Close claimed there was a conspiracy on the part of the Crown to convict George. His confession to Goddard and Moodie were to save them "from anything that would be disagreeable or threatening or adverse to them and their friends". In his summing up, Justice Backhouse declared that the idea Dean had made a confession to save Mr Goddard and his friends was the "most marvellous hypothesis" he had ever heard of.

The jury took just twenty minutes to reach their verdict: Guilty. Surely the jurors – as well as the population of Sydney and further afield – had been convinced of his guilt well

George cast a dejected figure as he sat in the dock during the trial.

before the trial started.

Acting Justice Backhouse reserved sentencing.

On the following morning George again stood trial, this time for perjury committed during his original trial The indictment was signed by Attorney-General Want who was present in court and conversed with the Judge as the indictment was read out. George pleaded not guilty.[12] Although Want was trying to distance himself from the conspiracy trial, he was very keen to be associated with the conviction of George Dean.

Again Colonna Close argued to Acting Justice Backhouse that the Royal Pardon covered evidence given by George while in the witness box, and again Backhouse dismissed his claim but reserved the point.

William Goddard and Richard Smith again gave evidence, much as they had on the previous day. Chimney sweep George Baker created some mirth when he described his profession as "Chimney Doctor". William Hamlet, the Government Analyst, stated he had analysed the soot taken from Dean's chimney by Baker and found arsenic in it. And George addressed the jury, restating the claims he made the day before.

In his summing up to the jury, Backhouse stated it was only due to the seriousness of the case, that he really feel a need to address them – the case was that simple.

"In reference to Mr Goddard's evidence," Backhouse said, "the law in that connection was that if anything was said, which could be construed in any way into a promise or an inducement or a threat, the statement made afterward by an accused person was inadmissible." And the Crown had now agreed to withdraw Goddard's evidence.

This time the jury took just under an hour to reach their verdict: Guilty.

Acting Justice Backhouse handed down his sentencing for the two trials, the maximum in each case: five years for swearing a false statement, and fourteen years for committing perjury during his trial, the sentences to be served concurrently.

"Thank you, Your Honour," George said. "Does that mean five years fully or fourteen years fully?"

"Fourteen years"

Colonna Close intended to appeal to the High Court on the reserved point of the free pardon.

The usual penalty for perjury was seven years but, if given during cases involving the death penalty, it doubled to fourteen years. Certainly George's sentence was harsh in that, clearly, the double penalty had been aimed at those giving evidence that could result in the hanging of an innocent man, rather than the man on trial lying in hope of preventing his hanging. At the same time, fourteen years was quite lenient relative to his original sentence of life imprisonment.

Several women, probably from the Konnecke family, burst into tears at the announcement of the guilty verdict. As George was being escorted from the dock, they clasped his hands. Brother William, sobbing and trembling, leaned over the rail, flung his arms around George and kissed him.[13]

11.

Conspiracy

Do we really want fair trials? No, we do not. We want justice, and quickly. And justice is whatever we deem it to be on a case-by-case basis.

Rogue Lawyer by John Grisham

The conspiracy trial would prove to be most bitter and acrimonious, particularly between Attorney-General John Want and Paddy Crick, and to a somewhat lesser extent between Want and Meagher. All three were politicians, Want a Government minister, Crick and Meagher with the opposition – Meagher had already resigned. One way or another, Want was intending to inflict as much damage as he could on Crick, who could be a verbal Rottweiler. As the saviour of Ernst Büttner from the death penalty in 1889, Crick had carried great clout as he lambasted Want during the agitation for the Dean Royal Commission, particularly on the point that Want, while holding the position of Attorney-General, had personally taken charge of Dean's prosecution in the courtroom, and could then take a prosecutorial bias into the cabinet room to have Dean executed rather than the sentence commuted.

Want was merciless in retribution. While the charge against Meagher could well be sustained, there was no evidence – other than suspicion – that Crick knew of Dean's confession. And this would be clearly shown as the conspiracy trial proceeded. Want had ordered arrest warrants be taken out against both Meagher and Crick, when the usual practice in such conspiracy cases – for men of their standing having no previous criminal offence – was simply to issue summonses requiring their attendance in court. At the remand hearing, Want had asked the Police Prosecutor to deny bail for Crick and Meagher and that they be kept in gaol until the trial – this was unheard of in such cases, particularly as no evidence of their guilt was tendered to the court – but the magistrate refused the demand. Instead he imposed enormous amounts of bail, at police request, far above any comparable conspiracy trial – £3,000 for Crick. Subsequently, Crick managed to get the bail reduced to £300. Until bailed the two accused had been kept at separate police stations in an attempt to prevent any communication between them (and Dean had been kept in isolation for the same reason).

Crick accused Want of a political conspiracy.

The committal hearing of the conspiracy case opened on October 30 – the Wednesday following Dean's conviction – at the Water Police Court before Stipendiary Magistrate Whittingdale Johnson and would sit for a lengthy nine days. Dick Meagher, Paddy Crick, George Dean, Daniel Green and Jane Reynolds were all present with their lawyers, apart from Crick who was representing himself. Crick was also suffering badly from influenza. As the only accused not bailed, George Dean sat in the dock while the other accused sat at tables with their lawyers.

Prosecutor Heydon spent the morning outlining the case, and tying together the alleged involvement of the five accused of conspiracy.

William Drake and Samuel Johnson, recorders of the

parliamentary Hansard record, produced speeches by Crick and Meagher in the house. Crick challenged their accuracy, getting them to admit there were errors in the reporting – not glaring errors, but errors nevertheless.

Crick strongly objected to speeches by Want and Salomons, given in Parliament under parliamentary privilege, being read out during this trial, saying this was being done to avoid any cross-examination of these witnesses by the defence on this evidence – a complete denial of the right of the accused. He had no objection to his own speeches being read out in this court (as he could be cross-examined on them). What Attorney-General Want had said of him in the House, Crick persisted, was a tissue of lies; as well as not appearing in the witness box himself in this trial, Want would not allow Salomons and Pilcher to appear; Want was trying to make "a football of justice".[1] Robert Levien, representing Dick Meagher, also objected to the absence of Sir Julian from the witness box. Despite these objections, Magistrate Johnson admitted the speeches as evidence.

Prosecutor Heydon also tried to introduce, as evidence, a newspaper report of the case. Crick again objected, on the ground that he could not cross-examine the newspaper – Magistrate Johnson refused its admission.[2]

Throughout the hearing, Crick strongly maintained, firstly, that he had believed entirely in Dean's innocence while he campaigned for the Royal Commission; secondly, that he had never spoken with Dean about the case, Meagher had handled the case solely.

Charles Collins, MLA, told the court that Crick had always stated to him that Dean was an innocent man, and he regarded Crick as a "truthful man".[3] At the time of the Royal Commission, relations between Crick and Meagher were strained and Crick had spoken of a possible dissolution of the partnership. Crick complained that Meagher took too much upon himself and did not consult him (as the senior partner).

Warder James Quain deposed that Meagher had visited Darlinghurst Gaol on April 9, and spoke with Dean in a corridor for over an hour with Quain out of earshot. The Darlinghurst gatekeeper, John Rose, gave the dates on which Meagher visited Dean, and stated there was no record of Crick, Green or Reynolds ever visiting Dean. Solicitor John Williams stated he was a member of the Dean Committee; he had never seen Crick at any of their meetings or at the Royal Commission; Crick and Meagher had only spoken at the public meetings when called upon to do so by the crowd.[4]

At 2:15 on November 2, following the lunch adjournment, George, the only accused under police restraint, complained to the Magistrate that no lunch had been provided for him, and he had not eaten since 6:30 am at the Gaol. While admonishing Gaol officials, the Magistrate continued the hearing and George went hungry.

Dr Newmarch, William Hamlet, William Goddard, Robert Moodie, Mary Dean, Richard Smith, Rose Kemp, Alexander Weyton, Inspector Cotter and Sergeant Brennan all gave evidence much as they had elsewhere.

Finally, on November 8, following passionate addresses by all the relevant lawyers representing their clients, and by Prosecutor Heydon, Magistrate Johnson committed the five accused for trial.

On the day Daniel Green surrendered to police (October 15), a second charge of conspiracy to pervert the course of justice had been brought against him. Crick had been engaged to defend Myra Heaven, a nurse also known as "Mrs H", who was accused of performing an illegal abortion on Jane Parkes, but passed the case on to Robert Levien after the conspiracy charges were brought against him.

A sworn statement had been made by Timothy Hill – who had been living with Parkes and was a witness in the case – that Green had paid him £10 to go to Brisbane (to make him unavailable as a witness). Hill did appear in the trial but refused to give evidence on the ground he was under arrest and could incriminate himself. After the jury retired to consider their verdict in the case, Crown Prosecutor Charles Wade (also involved in prosecuting the conspiracy case) examined Hill about Green after giving Hill immunity from prosecution on his answers. Hill admitted Green had met him in King Street in September. Yes, when he was arrested, he did tell Detective West that Green had given him £10 not to give evidence against Mrs Heaven – but he had lied to the detective, Green did not give him any money. Yes, he had made a sworn statement to the detective, but it was false. He could not remember what Green had said to him because he had been drinking. Yes, he had gone to Brisbane, but he had obtained the money for the fare by some illegal means, which he would not reveal. Yes, the vest and trousers he was wearing had been bought by Green.[5]

This examination by Wade, discrediting the only evidence against Green on the second charge, took place on October 10 – yet they persisted with the charge on October 15.

On October 26, Green was arrested again and a third charge made against him – that of assaulting Ellen Parker on September 4, causing her serious injury; that he was trying to persuade her not to appear as a witness in another case. Green's solicitor demanded that the police proceed with this case immediately, as he had court records to prove the innocence of his client. The Police Prosecutor insisted on a remand instead, and it was granted. Following this, each time Green appeared in court, the police demanded he be remanded again – on October 15, 22, 25, 29 and November 5 – keeping him locked up in gaol. Finally, on November 12 the court dealt with these matters. Police advised they were dropping the second charge involving Timothy Hill, but proceeded with the assault charge. Ellen Parker and her son, aged 13, deposed that Green had offered her £10 not to give evidence in a divorce case, and had then assaulted her when she refused the offer. Green deposed that he had never seen the woman until he was placed in a line-up at the police station after his arrest, and that he had no interest in that divorce case. The arresting officer admitted to the court that the description of Green, originally given to police by Parker and her son, in no way matched Green. Solicitor Ernest Gardiner testified that Green was with him, in court, at the time of the alleged assault. The Magistrate dismissed the case against Green, saying it was case of mistaken identity.[6]

In the newspapers the next day, Green bitterly complained that when arrested on the Mrs H charge – despite the lone witness Hill having previously recanted the evidence against him in a court of law – the Crown Prosecutor had asked that bail be refused and, when this was denied, had then sought a bail of £2,000, which was denied. When arrested on the assault charge, he told the police he had been in court at the time of the alleged assault. They checked it out, and knew all along that he was innocent, yet they persisted with the remands – to keep him in gaol – and finally brought him before the court on a charge they knew would fail (trying to justify his retention in gaol).[7]

Conspiracy

Daniel Green. Despite knowing full well that Green was innocent of all their charges against him, police demanded – five times – that Green, aged 26, should be remanded in gaol without bail, keeping him locked up for four weeks. The court released him, clearly innocent – it indicated political interference from above.

For Green, Crick and friends, these prosecutions had been all about political interference coming down from above – portraying Green in a bad light before the conspiracy trial (and reflecting badly on his accused co-conspirators) but also hoping Green might crack under the pressure and make injurious statements about Crick and Meagher. Henry Clarke MLA rose in parliament and asked the Minister for Justice a series of questions about these proceedings, but received a blank refusal to answer.

In 1895, Daniel Green was aged twenty-six and had been attending sheep and wool classes at Sydney Technical College. In March he had gone to Brewarrina, attending to family business with the Land Board there. He read about the Dean trial while there and on his return to Sydney, on April 20, contacted Meagher, who he knew, and joined the Dean Defence Committee. He worked closely with Meagher, including his election campaign. He also ran an errand for Meagher outside of the Dean issue (witness Hill) on at least one occasion. Green said these things he did for Meagher were on an entirely unremunerated, voluntary basis; he had also been a guest at the Meagher family home for Sunday dinner.[8]

And one would think that some of Green's actions – particularly with Hill – bordered on witness tampering.

The conspiracy trial opened on December 2 before Acting-Justice Henry Cohen and sat daily until December 19. It had been expected that Chief Justice Sir Frederick Darley would take the case but he disqualified himself on the ground that Salomons had consulted him about the case. The indictment was read out: "That on March 8, 1895, at Sydney, in the colony of New South Wales, the said prisoners did conspire amongst themselves to pervert the course of justice." A second indictment was virtually the same as the first. Barrister Richard O'Connor, representing Paddy Crick, objected to the generality of the charges against his client, saying there were a hundred different ways in which justice could be perverted - by suborning witnesses, by interfering with the verdicts of juries, by obtaining the escape of an accused, and so on – and fairness demanded the Crown state *how* justice had been perverted. Mr Justice Cohen did not accept the argument. March 8, the date of the said conspiracy, was the day Dean was arrested.

In selecting twelve jurors, each of the accused rejected their entitlement of 8 jurors, while the Crown rejected 14, making a total of 54 rejections. Realising the difficulty of finding men who had not formed an opinion about the case owing to its national, sensational nature, 96 potential jurors had been on standby at the court.

Most of the witnesses in this trial had given evidence about the case at other times. But there was one new witness on the first day who created a major stir. This was John Norton from the

John Norton. His *Truth* weekly newspaper became Australia's first tabloid newspaper, specialising in nasty divorces and seamier stories that mainstream newspapers would not print. Most of his testimony in the witness box consisted of extremely dubious one-on-one conversations. He was wily enough to avoid any charge of perjury.

Truth, a weekly newspaper which had been started in 1890 by William Willis, Paddy Crick and several other men – the intention had been to expound their political views but it soon developed into a racy tabloid newspaper under the editorship of Adolphus Taylor with Norton as Assistant Editor. In court, Norton claimed to be a friend of Meagher but admitted he had been at odds with Crick. It soon became obvious that this was deeply personal to Norton and his sole intention was to damage Crick as much as possible.

Norton told the court he had attended a Sunday lunch at Meagher's house after he was committed for trial – with the intent of gaining admissions from Meagher about Crick. Daniel Green was also there but he had asked that Green be sent away while he spoke privately with Meagher for two hours. He asked Meagher why he had allowed Crick "to crawl on top" of him, and how Crick managed to "extort" a sworn confession out of him. If Meagher had sought his advice, he would not have fallen into Crick's "trap". Meagher said that Crick believed both of them could be convicted, and that Meagher needed to make the confession so he (Crick) would not be convicted. Crick would break the partnership but treat him fairly, money wise, but Meagher would get nothing if he did not confess.⁹

Norton said he then questioned Meagher as to when Crick knew of Dean's guilt. Did Crick know it on the same day Meagher got the confession from Dean? Meagher did not answer him. Did Crick know it when moving the Royal Commission? Meagher did not answer. Did Crick know at the Town Hall meeting, when he was very drunk? Meagher said, "Yes, he did." How long before that night? Meagher said, "Many weeks before." Did Green know of Dean's guilt? Green knew nothing about it.

"It is not evidence against Crick or Green," Judge Cohen said.

"Have you seen Meagher since," Prosecutor Heydon asked.

"Yes, several times," Norton replied. "I have had several conversations, and Meagher told me that Crick knew of the guilt of Dean immediately after he obtained it from Dean."

"I shall ask Your Honour to rule whether this is evidence against Crick," Barrister O'Connor (for Crick) asked.

"From beginning to end, there is no word used which is evidence against Crick," His Honour replied. "I don't think there are more than three or four lines out of all that has been said that can go to the jury."

In his cross-examination of Norton, Barrister O'Connor clearly established Norton's detestation of Crick. In answering questions, Norton was evasive, argumentative and exhibited lapses of memory – he was very trial savvy. But he did admit that Crick had been responsible for his sacking as editor of the *Truth*; that Crick had been responsible for him suffering a prosecution for stealing money from the *Truth*; that Crick had sued him about a breach of an agreement; that he owed Crick £160 as a result of Crick winning that court case, but had no intention of paying him; that he had approached the

Attorney-General after Meagher's committal and asked to give evidence in this trial.

O'Connor questioned Norton about a conversation he had with a clerk named Cunningham, who had once worked for Crick. At first Norton could not remember any such conversation. Did he not ask Cunningham if he thought Crick knew of Meagher's guilt? Norton replied that he may have done so. Did not Cunningham say to him that he believed Crick did not know? Norton could not remember. Did he not then say to Cunningham that he agreed with him, that Crick did not know? No, Norton said, he could not remember any such thing.

While it was a highly sensational story for the newspapers, Norton's evidence had been a waste of the Court's time. It was uncorroborated, hearsay evidence from a man who obviously bore Crick great malice. As he was leaving the witness box, Norton confirmed this malice by threatening: "I shall settle with the man [Crick] who has attempted to swindle me and imprison me."

Meagher also cross-examined Norton and established that Norton had continually denied to him, including the day before the trial commenced, that he would be giving evidence in the trial. The clear intention of Norton's appearance as a witness in the trial, for both the prosecution and Norton, was to smear Crick.

The prosecution strongly contended that an integral part of the conspiracy had been Meagher interfering with prime Crown witness William Gail – who had passed the bottle of lemon syrup to Dr Newmarch resulting in the finding of its arsenic content – by having him arrested in April, just before Dean's first trial, in an effort to either obtain his non-appearance in that trial or to discredit him as a witness. Amelia Gail had obtained a divorce nisi from husband William in May 1892 on the grounds of his adultery.[10] Despite the Judge setting a period of three years before he could remarry, William had married Lydia just twelve months after his divorce, technically committing bigamy. Reading about her former husband's re-marriage during the Dean committal hearing, Amelia had approached Meagher in his office. He took her to the Police Station and a warrant was issued for Gail's arrest.

Sergeant Brennan deposed that he had subsequently interviewed Amelia Gail. She told him that after reading about the Dean case in the papers, she thought Meagher was the best solicitor to engage. Magistrate Francis Isaacs, who had signed Gail's arrest warrant at Central Criminal Court, deposed that Meagher had approached him for the arrest warrant but he refused to sign one until he interviewed Amelia Gail. He had been reluctant to issue an arrest warrant (on such a trivial matter) until she told him that her former husband had poisoned his brother, and it had been hushed up. Replying in Cross-examination, Isaacs stated that Meagher had made no statements during his interview with Mrs Gail (this question was trying to make the point that she was not being manipulated by him). He thought Meagher had a client relationship with Mrs Gail, and he had always respected Meagher as a solicitor.

In the witness box, William Gail said he had never seen his wife's divorce papers and was unaware he was supposed to wait three years before remarrying. He also denied poisoning his brother. Under cross-examination, he reluctantly admitted that Want's office had paid solicitor Levien (currently representing Jane Reynolds) to sort the matter out in the courts. No charges against him resulted; he wed Lydia Gail a second time to legalise the marriage; he gave evidence in the Dean trial. The docket to pay Gail's legal fees was later produced in court; it was initialled by Want, approving the payment. Defence counsel pointed out the extraordinary nature of the Attorney-General approving payment of *defence* fees for a man charged with a crime.

There were numerous occasions throughout this lengthy trial when the defence counsels would object to witnesses relating what Attorney-General Want had said or done, and demand his presence in court to give the evidence personally. Rarely were these objections granted. And Want certainly had no intention of appearing in court and being cross-examined on his role and methods in the case.

The prosecution tended the speeches of Attorney-General Want and Sir Julian Salomons for admission to be read to the court, as well as speeches made in Parliament by both Crick and Meagher. Defence counsels immediately objected. While the prosecution later withdrew the Crick and Meagher speeches, the Want and Salomons speech documents were retained.

The Salomons document was crucial, and the defence objected to its admission on the grounds that Salomons was not giving this evidence in personal testimony. Heydon contended that Meagher had admitted that the statements contained in it were truthful when he said: "Sir Julian Salomons did become from me the repository of the secret which is substantially given by him in his statement read to the Legislative Council". Meagher objected to its admission on the ground that Salomons breached client privilege to obtain the information.

The point was that by presenting Salomons' evidence as a document, it became complete fact as it could not be cross-examined on any point contained in it nor on any related issue. Apart from the unedifying spectacle of a High Court judge

 Four of the five accused had been granted bail and, as such, sat at tables surrounded by their lawyers, while George cast a lonely figure in the dock.

being cross-examined in a witness box, there was another issue that the Attorney-General desired to avoid. Salomon, while struggling with his conscience on whether he would reveal his knowledge of Dean's guilt (obtained under privilege), had made an offer to Meagher to personally pay Dean £50 to leave the country. Meagher did not relay the offer to Dean, who later said that, if he had known at the time that his guilt was about to be revealed and the money was on offer, he would have taken it. Legally, the offer was quite questionable, especially for a Justice of the High Court, as it would have enabled Dean to escape the law.

Hesitating, at first, to admit these documents as evidence, Acting Justice Cohen returned to the court after lunch and ordered the admission of the Want and Salomons documents. Several days later their admission was again raised. He noted the objections and stated that if he was wrong to admit them, an appeal to the High Court would be successful, but if he failed to admit them, and that was a wrong decision, the prosecution had no recourse to the High Court.[11]

The prosecution brought fifty-seven witnesses before the court, newspaper reporters, parliamentary officials, law officials, policemen, as well as witnesses – including Mary Dean, chemist John Smith and the foreman of the jury at the Dean trial – who had previously given evidence in a trial or at the Royal Commission.

Charles Goodchap, a member of the Legislative Council, was one witness who had not previously given evidence. He deposed that he had met Crick at the races on Saturday afternoon, July 27 (Crick corrected the date to August 3, a fortnight after Meagher's fatal consultation with Salomons) and, together with several other racegoers, had chatted with him. Crick related to them a conversation he had just had with Sir Julian Salomons (whose office was next door to Crick's office):[12]

"You are aware that Dean is guilty?" Salomons asked Crick.

"You seem very sure about it," Crick replied. "How do you know?"

"I don't absolutely know, but it is not an improbable thing for a prisoner to confide in his attorney, and I thought it probable he had done so with you?"

Crick then told his listeners that he "began to chaff" Salomons about suggesting Dean was guilty, and that he "would put Meagher on to him". Crick said there was an attempt to get a guilty confession out of Dean and to give him money to get him out of the country. If Dean were to receive any money, he would help set him up in business, not send him abroad.

Cross-examined, Goodchap said he was convinced that Crick believed in Dean's innocence. Goodchap was asked by Barrister O'Connor if Crick mentioned that Salomons claimed Windeyer had mishandled Dean's trial. No, Crick did not. But he, himself, had such a conversation with Sir Julian about two nights after Salomons made his speech in the Legislative Council. "Had I been Attorney-General," Salomons had said to Goodchap, "I should have conceived it to be my duty to advise the release of Dean in consequence of the observations, the improper observations I think, of Judge Windeyer."

On the ninth trial day, the prosecution closed and Barrister O'Connor made a lengthy plea to the Judge that no real evidence had been presented to the court concerning Crick, and that his client should be discharged. Acting Justice Cohen denied O'Connor's plea, and on the tenth trial day, the defence opened with Crick in the witness box.

Crick deposed that Meagher had been his junior partner for four years; they had a large volume of cases and they kept them completely separate. Meagher had been out of town when notification of the Dean trial was brought on, and he had accompanied Meagher to Court on the first day. After that he took no interest in the case and only learned of Dean's conviction in the papers. He also read the editorials complaining of Judge Windeyer's handling of the trial. He told Meagher he would raise the Windeyer issue in Parliament, but wanted to know if Meagher had ever asked Dean if he was guilty. Meagher had replied he had no need as Dean had continually protested his innocence. Before proceeding against Windeyer, Crick told Meagher, he needed to know whether Dean was guilty or innocent, as he did not want to be made a fool if it turned out afterwards that Dean was guilty. Meagher went to see Dean and returned to Crick saying Dean protested that he had never bought or handled poison in his life. Crick then made his attack on Windeyer in parliament.

Crick said he did not attend any of the Dean agitation meetings other than the last one at the Town Hall. He had not intended to speak at that meeting but, after the crowd caught sight of him, there were repeated calls for him to speak, and he said a "few words", which were fully reported.

Following the appointment of the Royal Commission, he argued with Meagher about "the conduct of the commission and [the] instruction of the counsel". He wanted Windeyer in the witness box at the Commission but Meagher did not. He said to Meagher: "If you are going to remain my partner, you will have to be guided by me."[13] The Windeyer issue was then left to Barrister Pilcher, a counsel to the Commission, and he refused to bring Windeyer into it. After that, Crick said, he had nothing to do with the Royal Commission (either organising witnesses or attending the hearing). On dissolving the partnership with Meagher, he paid him £1,500.

Dick Meagher followed Paddy Crick into the witness box. There seemed to be an impression, Meagher deposed, that he had a disposition to attack Judge Windeyer, but this was not true. He went into the Dean trial with no prejudice against Windeyer. The first time he appeared for the defence in a trial conducted by him, Windeyer had complimented him on the ability he had shown. But during this trial, Windeyer was very hostile to Dean – anything said in Dean's favour was passed over, anything detrimental was emphasised. In summing up, Windeyer distorted or passed over points that were favourable to Dean. He believed the trial was an outrage of justice, and still held that view (despite Dean's guilt). Windeyer may have been "accidently right" in the Dean trial (to believe Dean was guilty), but there may have been other trials where he was "accidently wrong" (to believe the accused was guilty). Following Dean's conviction, the newspaper reports were all about the "unsatisfactory character" of the trial, not about Dean being innocent. When he became aware of Dean's guilt, the agitation for a Royal Commission was well under way; if he had died at that moment, it would still have gone ahead.[14]

Sir Julian gained the knowledge of Dean's confession when they were in a client-counsel relationship; it should have remained sacred and he should never have revealed it. He never saw Mrs Reynolds until the Commission started; he was the one who suggested she go to the hospital to see if she could identify Mrs Dean. Daniel Green had never been in the employ of the Crick and Meagher law firm. He asked Green to go to Dean and tell him Sir Julian knew something about the case, and that was all Green knew; Green asked him if Dean would understand the message, and he replied that Dean would. It was Dean who sent Green on a message to chemist Smith. John Norton was a man of venom. He had much litigation with Crick and held great malice towards him. Norton had failed to get any statements incriminating Crick from him and had then "retailed a parcel of lies" to the court.[15]

Daniel Green deposed that he was in Brewarrina during the Dean trial, and people in the country were scandalised at the conduct of Judge Windeyer. He joined the Dean Defence Committee and worked actively for Dean. He did not understand the message Meagher gave him to take to Dean. Dean was ill and wrote a letter which he then took to Smith. Smith said: "You tell Dean if he does not see me for a couple of nights not to be afraid. I've stood the test so far, and I'm not likely to go back on him for anybody or anything." Meagher was annoyed that he had gone to Smith. A man named Delaney had told him about Mrs Reynolds, and he had gone into the hotel, showed her some photographs, and Mrs Reynolds had picked out Mrs Dean. He accompanied Mrs Reynolds to the hospital where she identified Mrs Dean. He had been actively engaged with Mr Meagher during his election campaign, and with him during the Royal Commission, but was not an employee of

Conspiracy

the law firm and never received a penny from them. He had gone into hiding because he saw there were heavy bails being awarded and he waited until he had the ability to lodge bail.[16]

George Dean declared that some of the things he said to Goddard and Moodie in his cell were not true, as he had been "driven completely insane". He was the one who sent Green to Smith. When he said Meagher had advised him to keep the secret, this was not true either.

Jane Reynolds deposed that she still believed that the woman who came to her hotel was Mrs Dean, although Mrs Dean was thinner than that woman. In cross-examination, she was asked if she still maintained her belief it was Mrs Dean. "To my mind it is," she replied, "I may be mistaken." Charles Knilands, a cabman, deposed that he had picked up a woman near Madam Rose's at that time, and driven her to Mrs Reynold's hotel; the woman looked very much like Mrs Dean.

At the beginning of the thirteenth trial day, the day after Crick had spent hours in the witness box, the foreman of the jury handed Judge Cohen an astonishing note: the jury wished to acquit Crick immediately as they firmly believed he had no knowledge of Dean's guilt until Meagher made his confession. Prosecutor Heydon objected and a discussion between counsels and the Judge ensued. The jury retired briefly and, on their return, confirmed their desire to acquit. His Honour accepted their decision and asked the formal questions. The foreman replied: "We find Mr Crick not guilty." The courtroom erupted to great applause.

"I think the verdict is a just one," Judge Cohen said, "and it is one in which I fully concur."

"I thank you for your kind remarks, Your Honour," Crick said.

"It is not mere kindness," the Judge replied. "It is simply justice."

With only a few days before the proroguing of parliament, Crick immediately returned to the Legislative Assembly and viciously attacked the character of Attorney-General Want. In the Legislative Council, Want returned fire on Crick in like manner. One newspaper commented that the two men, "like a pair of dogs on opposite sides of a fence, snarled and yapped and gnashed teeth at one another."[17] The broadsides ended with Want's departure for Japan the day after Parliament closed.

The trial continued into its final stage with counsels for the defence giving their addresses to the jury followed by Prosecutor Heydon. On the sixteenth and last day of the trial, Acting Justice Cohen spent nine hours addressing the jury. The jury retired at 6:30 pm and returned at 9:00 with their verdict:

Daniel Green: not guilty.

Jane Reynolds: not guilty.

George Dean: Guilty.

Richard Meagher: Guilty with a recommendation to mercy.

A woman's scream rent the court; it was Alice Meagher, Dick's wife, who was then helped from the court as she broke down sobbing.

Dick Meagher and Colonna Close (for Dean) immediately notified the Judge of their intention to appeal the verdict. Judge Cohen said he would defer sentencing until after the appeal was heard. George Dean returned to his Darlinghurst cell and Dick Meagher was given bail of £3,000 with two sureties of £1,500, one of whom was Paddy Crick.

12.

The Scales of Justice

> It didn't matter in terms of the strategy of the case whether the defendant did it or not. What mattered was the evidence against him – the proof – and if and how it could be neutralized. My job was to bury the proof, to colour the proof a shade of gray. Gray was the colour of reasonable doubt.
>
> **The Lincoln Lawyer by Michael Connelly**

The appeal against George Dean's convictions for perjury and swearing a false document came before the Full Court of Justice Henry Stephen and Justice Archibald Simpson on February 28, 1896, with Colonna Close again appearing for George, and Charles Wade opposing for the Crown. On the charge of swearing a false declaration, Close contended that it had been induced by Mr Goddard – the Judge agreed it had been induced – and Goddard was a person of authority. Wade contended that Goddard was not a person of authority. On the charge of committing perjury at his original trial, Close argued firstly, the royal pardon given to Dean precluded this charge and, secondly, the confession obtained by Goddard and Moodie was read to the jury and, although subsequently withdrawn, would have influenced the jury. After lengthy argument, the appeal was dismissed.

The appeal against the conspiracy convictions of Dean and Meagher opened on March 5 before the Full Court of Justice

Stephen, Justice Simpson and Justice Owen, with Barrister Edmund Barton representing Dick Meagher and Colonna Close again representing George Dean. Barton and Close presented a list of nineteen points to be argued. After two days the Court adjourned for two months until May 11.

The Court decided to approach the appeal by giving a decision after each point was argued. On the first point, Barton argued that the charge of conspiracy against the accused was too general or vague, it did not specify any overt acts of the alleged conspiracy (such as suborning a witness). Justice Stephen strongly agreed with this point but the other Justices disagreed – it was dismissed 2-1.[1]

The second point revolved around the admissibility of the speeches made in Parliament by Meagher, Crick, Want and Salomons. Barton firstly claimed that statements made in Parliament had absolute privilege and could not be used in a court of law, in particular Meagher's confession speech. Justice Stephen doubted this saying it would mean, for example, that a Member of Parliament could make a confession of murder in the House and it could not be used in his trial.[2]

Barton said the speeches of Want and Salomons had been read to the jury and six copies given to the jury (to be read at their leisure).

"They should never have been read to the jury or placed before them," Barton said.

"I feel that strongly," Justice Simpson said. "I read the whole of Sir Julian's long and undoubtable able speech last night … and it contains assertion after assertion about things said to have been done and said by Meagher."[3]

"And there was the colour in which the Attorney-General painted the conduct of Mr Crick," Barton said.

The Scales of Justice

"Is the effect of the statements made in them," Justice Simpson said, "to be got rid of simply by the Judge saying to the jury, 'You must not consider anything in these speeches unless Meagher had admitted that the statements or some of them were correct?'"[4]

In other words, Judge Cohen had directed the jury to ignore those parts of the speech that were not admitted to be true by Meagher. How were they to ignore what they read or heard in those speeches? Salomons, for example, had called Crick and Meagher "conspirators".

Justice Simpson stated that the speeches were not *sworn* testimony. Why were Want and Salomons not called to give their evidence in the trial where such testimony would be *under oath* and able to be *cross-examined*? He felt so strongly about the wrongful admission of these two speeches that, if the appeal was dismissed (he was out-voted), he would recommend that both the accused be given a pardon. (How ironic would it be if the Executive Council was requested to give Dean another pardon, albeit on this charge alone!)

Justice Owen agreed that the speeches were inadmissible.

Justice Stephen said there was no need for him to comment as he had upheld the appeal on the first point.

The appeal against Meagher's conviction was upheld unanimously.

Close had argued that no evidence had been presented throughout the trial on Dean's part in the alleged conspiracy and that his confession was inadmissible.

"The decision of the Court applies just as much to Dean as it does to Meagher," Justice Owen said. "If Meagher was improperly convicted, there was no one [left] for Dean to conspire with."[5]

The appeal against Dean's conviction was also upheld unanimously.

It was obvious that this conspiracy trial had been completely mishandled by Attorney-General Want. There would be no retrial, as conspiracy in this period was considered a misdemeanour (small sentencing), not a felony, and retrials could only be applied in felony cases. Crick, Green and Reynolds should never have been put on trial – there was simply no evidence against them. George Dean had simply lied in court and had already received fourteen years for perjury as punishment. Meagher, on the other hand, was certainly guilty of conspiracy to pervert the cause of justice – during the Royal Commission, he promoted and assisted the theory Mary Dean poisoned herself, knowing full well she did not – and had gotten off the charge on the technicality of inadmissible evidence, which Want had insisted be used.

While George Dean was returned to his Darlinghurst cell, Dick Meagher left the court a free man.

Two weeks later Dick Meagher appeared before High Court – consisting of Chief Justice Sir Frederick Darley, Justice Stephen and Justice Owen – to show cause why he should not be struck off the Roll of Solicitors. Barristers Barton and Gannon represented Meagher. Gannon read to the Court an affidavit written by Meagher consisting of thirty-two points, outlining his behaviour relative to the Dean case. Meagher contended that while he had made errors of judgement, his solitary aim had been his duty to his client.

Barton argued that Meagher had a *bona fide* belief of the injustice of the trial and that had formed his later behaviour – for example, the Judge had practically told the jury to convict Dean. There had been a strong wave of public opinion formed, not by Meagher or Crick, but by newspapers.

"The papers misreported what was done at the trial by making it appear that, [what] Mr Justice Windeyer had stated concerning the prisoner before the verdict, [was] what he said in passing sentence after the verdict," the Chief Justice said. "Of course Mr Meagher cannot be made responsible for the misreports of the press."[6]

In his affidavit, Barton continued, Meagher said he was "torn by conflicting emotions" after he discovered Dean's guilt. His decision to conceal it from Crick led him to later make false statements. If he had revealed Dean's guilt, he would have been portrayed as a lawyer who betrayed his client. Crick decided to bring the trial before Parliament after reading about it in the *Daily Telegraph*.

"Then the answer [of guilt] given by Dean should have been information for Crick as well as Meagher," Justice Stephen said.

"If he had told his own partner of the true state of affairs," Chief Justice Darley said, "then probably, he and his partner would have remained quiescent and done nothing, letting the public take what course they saw fit."

If Meagher held himself to be under a sacred obligation not to reveal Dean's guilt, Justice Stephen asked, why did he reveal it to Sir Julian Salomons?

Because he believed Salomons was under a similar sacred obligation not to reveal his disclosure, Barton replied.

Barton made a final plea that Meagher be treated leniently by the Court; he was a young man (just thirty) with a promising career ahead of him, and an otherwise unblemished record.

After adjourning and considering their decision, the Justices returned to the Court and the *Australian Star* reported the decision delivered by Chief Justice Darley: "Mr. Crick, the senior partner, wanted to ascertain whether Dean was guilty or innocent, and Meagher was requested to go to Darlinghurst and see Dean. Dean confessed; in other words he confessed that he was guilty of one of the most atrocious crimes that a human being could be guilty of, an attempt to murder his wife by administering slow poison to her. Respondent returned and saw his senior partner. Meagher not only suppressed the truth in this conversation with Crick, but made a deliberate misstatement, saying that Dean protested his innocence, and that he (Meagher) still believed him innocent. Crick, relying on his partner's solemn assurance, requested in Parliament that a Royal Commission should he appointed. Now Meagher would not be punished in this case for refusing to disclose a professional secret, but there was no reason why he should not have disclosed it to his own partner, as there would have been no breach of confidence in that. If he had disclosed it, they could readily believe that Crick would have advised him to remain quiescent so far as the agitation that was going on was concerned. But Meagher deceived his partner and led him to think that Dean was innocent. Alluding to the meeting in the Town Hall, which both members of the firm attended, His Honour said that they could quite understand Crick's speech, but Meagher said 'He was there to raise his voice on behalf of truth'. At this time he was aware that Dean was guilty of this crime … Did he ever consider what he was doing in endeavouring to obtain Dean's release? Did he not see that he was thereby fixing Dean's crime on innocent people, that he was charging Mrs Dean and her mother with an atrocious crime? … What would Meagher have done if Mrs. Dean and her mother had been arrested on the charge of conspiracy to bring about Dean's conviction?"[7]

Meagher was struck off in a unanimous decision.

The Scales of Justice

The phrase "Scales of Justice" refers to statues or sculptures of a woman – sometimes called Lady Justice, but derived from Justitia, the Roman Goddess of Justice – who is often blindfolded, to show her objectivity, holds a set of scales in one hand, to weigh the evidence, and a sword in the other hand, to punish the guilty. On one hand, the general community expects that a person committing a criminal offence should be brought before a court and given an appropriate punishment. On the other hand, the evidence should be carefully weighed in a *fair* trial i.e. it needs to be proved *beyond a reasonable doubt* that the person is guilty of the offence – it should not be sufficient to simply *believe* in the person's guilt.

Ethically, a lawyer should not allow his client to lie under oath – lawyers have been known to withdraw from cases on this issue. In consultations with clients who plead not guilty, it is usual for lawyers to refrain from asking clients whether they are guilty or not, and this then allows the lawyer to simply deal with the evidence of the case presented by the prosecution.

In modern times, author John Mortimer, a British barrister, created the character Horace Rumpole, an Old Bailey (London Central Criminal Court) solicitor, in a series of books. In a story titled "The Scales of Justice", Rumpole defends a policeman who had previously complained that the scales of justice had tipped too far in favour of the defendant. Rumpole uses his legal guile and the policeman is found not guilty. The policeman tells Rumpole that his tactics in his case were justifiable as he knew he was innocent. Rumpole replies: "I know no such thing. I hang up such thoughts when I don my wig. I present the best case I can, but leave the jury to decide guilt. It's their job, not mine."[8]

During the conspiracy trial, Crick deposed: "I asked him

[Meagher] if Dean had told him anything about his guilt … In my practice, I have never asked a man charged with a capital offence whether he was guilty or not whilst acting professionally for him, and, so far as I know, Mr Meagher has observed the same rule."[9]

It was generally accepted that Crick told the truth when he said he did not know of Dean's guilt until after Salomons' revelation of it. For Meagher though, there was a deep suspicion – and within much of the legal fraternity, it was strong belief – that Meagher knew of Dean's guilt *before* his trial. This resolved around Meagher's questioning of chemists appearing in Dean's committal hearing in March 1895, when William Guise, Arthur Street and Thomas MacDonald gave their evidence about scripts they filled for Mary. Meagher, in a brief cross-examination, asked each of those chemists if he had ever sold poison to Dean; each replied in the negative. The fourth chemist called was Richard Smith – Meagher did not ask him any questions.[10] Questioned about this in the conspiracy trial, Meagher weakly stated that he was not aware that Smith sold poison.

For Meagher to know of Dean's guilt and then, during the trial, claim Mary Dean and Caroline Seymour were possible originators of the poison would indeed be "monstrous" (as described by Judge Windeyer). Without the knowledge of Dean's guilt, it was a legitimate (though rather nasty) defence tactic for Meagher to offer an alternate possibility to Mary's poisoning.

As a client of Sir Julian Salomons, Meagher placed the highly respected barrister-judge in an invidious position. Salomons was torn between his duty to keep what passed between them sacrosanct, and the terrible knowledge that, not only had Mary Dean been poisoned by her husband, but she had been doubly victimised by Meagher's defence strategy of accusing her of poisoning herself, which was then accepted as true by much of the public, and led to Mary suffering so much acrimonious comment and jeering. Sir Julian's conscience won out and he made the revelation.

At the same time, Sir Julian believed Dean had not received a fair trial. He told both Paddy Crick and Charles Goodchap privately: "Guilty or innocent, Dean should have been released, because of the conduct of the judge at the trial."[11]

There were a number of issues that made the trial of George Dean *unfair*.

- Throughout the trial, suspicion was often treated as proof. The high circumstantial evidence of Mary's poisoning was that George was the only other adult in the house. Yet there was much that pointed to George being innocent: the prosecution could not prove that he had poison in his possession; they could not provide a motive for the crime other than minor squabbles with his wife of twelve months; and people were lining up in droves to vouch for his high character, not to mention his heroic rescues of passengers fallen overboard from his ferry. Suspicion that he had previously poisoned meals made by Caroline, which tasted awful and had been thrown out, were treated as actual poisonings by Judge Windeyer. While George was suspected of placing poison in the lemon syrup, the bottle had passed through a number of hands before finally reaching the Government Analyst, opening the possibility that the poison could have been added by someone other than George.
- False forensic evidence was given to the jury – that arsenic and strychnine counteracted each other – and its

falseness was confirmed in the Royal Commission. In the 1890s a conviction could not be appealed on the grounds of false evidence, only on technical legal points in the administration of the trial.
- Justice Sir William Windeyer, the trial judge, removed his impartial blindfold and clearly showed his bias, particularly in his second address to the jury.

Attorney-General John Want decided to personally prosecute Dean, raising the profile of the case. His reasons were more personal and political than that of justice. In his summing up to the Dean jury, his main point had been that if Dean did not poison his wife, who did? He suffered great criticism in Crick's campaign for a Royal Commission, and Want's instigation of the conspiracy trial was purely vindictive, aimed to at least smear Crick in particular, and Meagher to a lesser extent. Crick's early not guilty verdict by the jury defeated that utterly, and rebounded on Want.

Dick Meagher had approached Sir Julian Salomons for legal advice, miffed that the *Daily Telegraph* had accused him of mishandling Dean's trial. Yet there was some justification for such criticism of Meagher. He baldly accepted the forensic evidence presented by the prosecution, and did not seek a second opinion which, provided at the Royal Commission, contradicted it. He did not offer accidental poisoning as an alternative to George being the poisoner. There had been cases of arsenic, a tasteless white powder easily confused with flour and widely held for vermin poisoning, accidently placed in food, then sold or given to someone – although this usually resulted in more than one person being poisoned. Meagher also put George into the witness box where he could be cross-examined. After the trial, members of the jury stated that they had believed completely in his innocence until that point in the trial (they then asked to hear Mary give her evidence again). Admittedly, this was the first decade in which the accused could enter the witness box in their own defence and, unlike modern times, some judges (Justice Windeyer was one) construed that defendants would only fail to enter the witness box if they were guilty.

Meagher was right to be greatly concerned that Dean had not received a fair trial. But he knew Dean was guilty after the trial (if not before). His greatest mistake was to conceal Dean's confession from his partner Crick – and Crick would have stepped back from the issue – and then to compound that blunder by attending meetings designed to establish a Royal Commission, and following that to participate in the Royal Commission. With knowledge of Dean's guilt, he should have let the newspapers take the issue where it would, and that may, or may not, have led to the establishment of the Royal Commission. If the Commission failed to eventuate, Meagher could at least be content with the knowledge that the man serving the prison sentence was not innocent.

So, what was Meagher's motive in lying to Crick? Back in 1889, two years before he became Paddy Crick's junior partner, Ernst Büttner, Crick's client, had been convicted and sentenced to hang. Crick had subsequently had the verdict quashed and obtained a free pardon for Büttner – all to great acclaim and the rise of his criminal legal firm to the largest in Sydney. Meagher clearly desired a similar acclaim.

Justice Sir William Windeyer was highly respected for his judgements in jurisprudence. But if, as a judge in a criminal trial, he formed a belief in the guilt of the accused, particularly if the victim was a female, he was prone to show it, highly concerned the jury might give the "wrong" verdict. The role of the judge in a trial is one of a legal referee, keeping both prosecution and defence to the rule of law and then, in a final address to the jury, explaining to these laymen the intricacies of law in connection with the evidence they have heard during the trial.

After the jury had been considering their verdict for four and a half hours, the foreman returned to the courtroom and asked Judge Windeyer if it was right for the majority to convince the minority of their verdict; Windeyer replied in the affirmative, and the foreman returned to the jury room. When the jury had still not reached a verdict after eight hours, Windeyer called them back into the court. The issues, he said, were so clear in the case that he must have failed in some way when he explained it to them; it would be a scandal if they could not reach a decision, unless they believed the "monstrous" idea that the woman had herself taken poison five times over. They could make a strong recommendation for mercy (indicating the accused may not be hanged). It was then Saturday night and, if they did not return a verdict by midnight, they would be locked up over Sunday until the Court resumed on Monday.

Could there be a doubt as to which verdict Judge Windeyer believed the jury should return?

The jury returned with their guilty verdict seven minutes later.

Not content to simply state his agreement with the verdict, as most judges did, Windeyer lashed Dean saying he knew he did it as if he had seen it with his own eyes. He then passed sentence of death and told Dean to prepare himself to meet his Maker. Windeyer would later defend this post-verdict lambast saying he did recommend to the Executive Council that Dean's sentence be commuted to life imprisonment. Secondly, he did not want to lock the jury up over Sunday as the son of the

Foreman had died and was to be buried on Sunday afternoon. This could well have been a compassionate motive for his second address to the jury, but it certainly came across as a threat.

In 1896, Windeyer travelled to England. He died in September 1897 in Italy. Following his death, a conversation he had with a friend about the Dean case, was published in Australian newspapers. Windeyer stated that as soon as he heard Mary give her evidence he became convinced she was telling the truth, and this was reinforced when George gave his evidence. He thought the jury also believed Mrs Dean, and he had recalled them "with the idea of clearing up any doubts they might have".[12]

In response, the *Evening News* editorialised: "Judge Windeyer, even in his most masterful and self-assertive moods on the bench, was not firmly persuaded that he was simply doing his duty. He was no doubt altogether unconscious that on such occasions his utterances were wholly destitute of the impartiality which should distinguish a judge. Never was there a more unfortunate display of those peculiar attributes of his than at the trial of Dean. That incident of the recalling of the jury and the second address to them – an address which, in whatever spirit it was meant, had far too near a resemblance to a command – was undoubtedly answerable for all the discreditable things which followed, and for the way in which justice itself seemed to be dragged in the mire. If Judge Windeyer had not suffered his impressions as to Dean's guilt to carry him away, and had not harangued the jury in the extraordinary style he did, Dean in all likelihood would have been convicted, and there would have been an end."[13]

Immediately after the trial, the Foreman of the jury had confirmed that, before being recalled by Windeyer, they were on the verge of convicting Dean.

Following the announcement of Dean's guilt, Windeyer attended a dinner in Adelaide and was congratulated on being right. During his reply he broke into sobs. The *Australian Star* reported: "[Windeyer] said for weeks past his back had been against the wall. The current of public feeling had been against him, and he had been represented as unjust and cruel. But through it all he had been sustained by the knowledge of his own integrity."[14]

While Windeyer may have felt vindicated at the news of Dean's guilt, it showed he just did not get it. If he had been completely impartial during the Dean trial, as justice required, it is almost certain the jury would have convicted Dean – and none of the ugly legal ructions that followed would have ensued.

There were many lessons to be learned from the Dean trial and its repercussions, not just for the legal participants, but for the legal profession as a whole.

On May 22, 1896, Mary sued George for divorce on the grounds of cruelty in that he had poisoned her with intent to murder. This posed a small legal problem in that George had been pardoned for that crime making him technically innocent. Mr Justice Simpson reserved judgement and brought the matter before the bench of the High Court four days later. The point was agued through by Mary's barrister and common sense prevailed in its acceptance by the Court. Justice Simpson granted a decree nisi, the divorce becoming absolute after three months on September 1.

Four years later, on a wet miserable Wednesday evening at St Peter's Presbyterian Church in North Sydney – June 6, 1900 – Mary married a second time. In a desire to keep the wedding as quiet as possible, there had been no publicity, yet reporters were present. And it was certainly a wedding vastly different from her first to George Dean, when her mother was the only witness. The *Australian Star* reported that there were between 60 and 70 guests waiting inside the church as the bride and groom arrived in separate hansom cabs.

The *Star* continued: "Tastefully-gowned in a biscuit-coloured merveilleux silk, with hat to match, and attended by three little bridesmaids, the bride entered the church leaning on the arm of the friend by whom she was to be given away. The bridegroom was Mr Benjamin William Bridge, described in the declaration as 'a bachelor of Annandale'. The ceremony over, the party retired to the vestry, from which they made their exit a few minutes later to be greeted with showers of rice, rose-leaves and confetti."[15]

There was one child born in what appears to have been quite a happy marriage, a boy named John (usually called Jack) in 1902.

Caroline Seymour died on December 28, 1921, at her daughter's residence in the Sydney suburb of Punchbowl. The *Sydney Morning Herald* recorded her passing in its "Deaths" column as "Caroline Asbury, dearly loved mother and mother-in-law of Ben and Mary Bridge, and loving grandma of Breta and Jack."[16] Her age was given as eighty-nine.

Caroline had given baby Florence the nickname of Breta as she nursed her while Mary was recovering from the effects of her poisoning – the name came from Breta Holmes, the daughter of Captain Holmes and his wife, good Newcastle friends known to Caroline and Mary from before Mary met George.[17]

Mary lived a long life, dying at Gosford in 1969 at the age of ninety-five.

Epilogue

Character on Trial

But never mind, the time will come
When I once more will be free to roam under the sun;
And then all laws must from me cease,
And by that time I hope I will be able to live at ease.
George Dean (written while on trial)

Paddy Crick had married Mary Kelly in 1890, but became estranged from her two years later. Although no longer sharing a bedroom, they continued to live in the same house, with Crick often living for long periods in a hut down the back yard. He had a constant battle with his gambling and drinking addictions. Rated as Sydney's biggest gambler, and regularly racking up huge losses, he owned champion horses and drank in racing circles when away from parliament. His declaration in 1903 that he was giving up drinking and smoking came to nothing. When Sir John See retired as Premier in 1904, he nominated Crick as his successor, but the Governor, Sir Harry Rawson, rejected him on the ground of his excessive drinking at Executive Council meetings.

Crick served as Secretary for Lands from 1901 to 1904, and this would prove to be his downfall. Following a change of government, a Royal Commission was set up in 1905 to investigate the administration of the Lands Department under

Epilogue

Crick. It found that Crick had overruled the adverse reports of his department and awarded leases on thirty-five occasions through agents who received large commissions. His mate William Willis was the agent in twenty-one cases and Peter Close with nine. The Commissioner firmly believed that Crick had been receiving kick-backs (or bribes) from these men, and Crick stood trial at Central Criminal Court on March 22, 1906. The two indictments accused Crick of receiving £250 bribes from Close on two separate occasions. Close gave evidence that Crick had warned him that he wanted nothing illegal to do done in connection with their land leases, and that the £250 payments were for road constructions. The trial ended suddenly when Prosecutor Shand admitted he had insufficient evidence to convict Crick, who was then found not guilty. The *Australian Star* wondered why Crick had been put on trial with so little evidence, and the Royal Commissioner was yet to complete his investigation. Crick had business dealings with Close and many others connected to the leases, making it difficult to determine whether or not the payments to him were bribes or business payments. But the Commission could not find where Close's payments had entered into the Lands Commission's complex accounts.

On May 23, the interim report of the Royal Commission was issued by Justice Owen, condemning Crick and Willis.

On November 13, 1906, Crick, along with William Willis and Charles Bath, was again charged with conspiracy (over alleged payments to him). After sitting fifteen days, the jury acquitted Bath but could reach no agreement on Crick and Willis. Six jurymen complained to Attorney-General Charles Wade of "misconduct" in the jury room by two of the Sherriff's officers (who were seen immediately after the trial to be dining with Jim Crick, brother of Paddy) in dealing with the jury, and a juryman who, at the beginning of the trial, declared that he would find the accused innocent no matter what, and proceeded to do so. A Royal Commission was established and quickly found that the officers were not guilty of misconduct.[1] The juryman was charged with contempt of court and brought before the Full Court of three Justices, who admonished him, but declined any punishment saying what happened in the jury room was sacrosanct.[2]

On December 7, 1906, the Premier moved a motion requesting Crick to attend parliament and answer questions raised by the Royal Commission. A letter, containing Crick's resignation, was immediately handed to the Speaker read out by him. Five days later, despite his resignation, the Premier moved a motion that Crick be formally expelled from parliament: "That in view of the findings of the Royal Commissioner, which have been read to this House, the said William Patrick Crick is adjudged guilty of conduct which should render him ineligible to sit as a member of this Assembly." The motion carried by voices.[3]

On July 26, 1906, the Legislative Assembly had first adopted a resolution that Crick be suspended from the House "until the verdict of the jury had been returned in the criminal trial now pending, or until it is further ordered."[4] Ignoring the resolution, Crick took his seat in the House. Ordered to leave by the Speaker, Crick refused, and the Sergeant-at-Arms ejected him on the Speaker's order. Crick charged both the Speaker and the Sergeant-at-Arms with assault, outrageously suing each for £2,000 in damages, and claiming the Assembly did not have the power to suspend him. The matter came before the Full Court, headed by Chief Justice Cohen, in February 1907. The

Epilogue

Court gave a majority judgement to Crick. The Sergeant-at-Arms (with the Government's support) appealed to the Privy Council in London, which upheld his appeal.

The re-trial of Crick and Willis began on April 9, 1907, with Charles Pilcher leading the prosecution and Crick defending himself. For the first time, the accused were not given bail but locked up in gaol at night time – Crick objected strongly to being locked up with criminals. Peter Close again gave evidence. The trial dragged on into May. A man, who owned a shop near the gaol, provided meals three times a day for the accused and, on at least one occasion, emptied ginger beer bottles and filled them with alcoholic spirits. On May 7, after the Judge had summed up for seventeen hours, the jury retired and once again were unable to reach a verdict. The Attorney-General announced there would be no further prosecution of Crick and Willis.

Just ten days later, Justice Owen handed down the final report of the Royal Commission, and was unequivocal in deciding that half of Close's commission fee had gone to Crick as a bribe (about £8,000).

The deepest cut was yet to come.

On August 6, 1907, Crick was brought before the Full Court to show cause why he should not be removed from the legal roll and disbarred from practicing as a lawyer. Three weeks later, the seven Justices announced their decision, with one Justice dissenting – that Crick be struck off.[5] Nothing could have hurt Paddy Crick more.

Crick immediately began campaigning for the Sydney seat of Surrey Hills but was easily defeated in the September election, giving finality to his severance from law and government.

Paddy Crick died on August 23, 1908, due to cirrhosis of

the liver and was buried in the Catholic section of Waverly Cemetery – he was just forty-six. Towards the end, his mother and father joined his estranged wife in the Crick household to care for him. As he died intestate and his marriage had been childless, the court awarded £5,200 to his wife and £4,700 to his father.

William Patrick Crick was a tragic figure of Shakespearian proportions. One of the best descriptions of this very talented man comes from author Cyril Pearl who, in his 1958 book, described him as an "accomplished demagogue" and wrote: "[Crick] looked like a prize fighter, dressed like a tramp, talked like a bullocky, and to complete the pattern of popular virtues, owned champion horses which he backed heavily and recklessly … He combined a remarkable knowledge of Parliamentary procedure with a complete contempt for the dignities and decencies of Parliament. He was uncontrollable in debate, defying Speaker or Chairman to silence him, and uninhibited in invective."[6]

At the general election, held on July 27, 1898, Dick Meagher stood for the seat of Tweed (although he lived in Bondi, Tweed held a large Irish constituency) and, much to the surprise of many, won by a large majority. He stood as an independent but two years later joined the Labor Party. While he was held in great odium by the conservative legal fraternity, from whom he would never receive forgiveness, it was becoming very clear that he never lost his popularity with the man in the street.

John Norton was also elected to the Legislative Assembly in these elections, but was opposed to Meagher. Two years earlier, Norton had become owner/editor of the weekly newspaper *Truth*. William Willis, who had started the paper as the major

Epilogue

owner (along with Paddy Crick and others), had been in great legal trouble over his publication of a certain letter. It was suggested that Norton probably gained control of the paper by blackmailing Willis on this issue. Following his takeover of *Truth*, its circulation certainly expanded greatly – especially with the working class – as he increased its spicy mix of sport, crime and scandal, particularly divorce cases, and showed irreverence to figures of authority. Norton also used *Truth* to great effect to lambast his political opponents.

On Sunday, September 11, 1898, Norton attacked the character of Dick Meagher in a lengthy article. In the next issue, Norton followed up with a longer and even more vicious and merciless assault, calling him "Mendax [Liar] Meagher" and describing him as "the premier perjurer of our public life and the champion criminal of this continent"[7] – over two pages of the *Truth*. Always thin-skinned when it came to personal attacks on him – and Norton, who dubiously claimed in the conspiracy trial to be his friend, would have been well aware of this – Meagher was outraged beyond control. On the following Thursday, carrying a whip, he waited for Norton to emerge from Her Majesty's Theatre in King Street. On sighting Norton, Meagher attacked him, knocking him to the ground and repeatedly striking him with the whip. Norton pulled a loaded pistol from his pocket and fired a shot at Meagher – apparently pre-warned of Meagher's intention to assault him. The shot missed Meagher, who dived behind a carriage, then made a swift departure by jumping into a passing hansom cab.

Both men were arrested and charged with assault. Appearing in court, both men cross-examined the other in what would prove to be one of the court's greatest verbal stoushes, both freely lashing the other with abuse and invective. At one stage, the Bench called police to clear the court. Eventually, Meagher was found guilty of assault but merely fined £5. Norton was acquitted on the ground that Meagher instigated the fracas and Norton was of a much smaller physique.

Throughout his career, Dick Meagher was a robust debater but (in contrast to Paddy Crick) mindful of court etiquette, treating judges and opposing counsel with respect and never using low language. He could sift through big issues, often using grandiloquent oratory with Greek or Roman references, but always using finely argued logic. In 1900, he was appointed a Royal Commissioner enquiring into William Creswell's claims in the notorious Tichborne affair – it was extraordinary for a disbarred solicitor to receive such an appointment. Meagher held the Tweed seat until 1904 when it was abolished under a redistribution. Absent from parliament for three years, he won the seat of Phillip in 1907 and held it for ten years.

Meagher's greatest desire was to return to the law, to use his immense skill and reap its rich rewards. His applications to the Full Court for re-admission to the legal rolls in 1900, 1902 and 1904 were all refused. He stated in his 1904 application that his disbarment so far had cost him £14,000 in legal fees. It was reported that Chief Justice Sir Frederick Darley thought a ten-year suspension would be sufficient punishment for Meagher, and he ought to reapply in 1906. The Full Court refused to hear his application for re-instatement in August 1906, when Willis and Crick were involved in the land scandal – while Meagher had been a land agent, the Royal Commission did not accuse him of any wrongdoing, and he ceased all land operations when the scandal broke.

A fifth application, made in July 1909 before the three members of the Full Court, was successful with a two-one

Epilogue

decision in his favour, and he was cheered from the Court. Three days later, he appeared at the Water Police Court defending a client. Vindictively, the Law Institute, appealed the decision. In November, the High Court unanimously reversed the decision after reading some of Meagher's land correspondence with Willis, but admitting the letters only made the Justices suspicious of misconduct on Meagher's part – it was guilt by association. After three months of legal practice, Meagher was again struck off the law books.

Over the next decade, the stature and popularity of Dick Meagher continued to grow. He rose in the Labor Party to become president in 1914. In 1912, it appeared that Meagher would be appointed to State Cabinet, but the Governor, Lord Chelmsford, indicated that he would not receive Meagher if such an appointment were made. He had been an alderman on the Sydney Municipal Council since 1901, and in January 1916 became the popular Lord Mayor of Sydney, serving for two years.

The issue of conscription for the war in Europe divided the nation; surprisingly, Meagher came out strongly in favour of conscription and was expelled from the Labor Party (along with several other members). He sat on the cross-bench as an independent, but still voting Labor on other issues. As Lord Mayor, he attended many committees and functions in support of Australian troops overseas, as well as recruitment rallies. In the bitter state election campaign in November 1916, Meagher ran as an Independent Labor candidate, but failed to regain the seat of Phillip. He supported the workers, as did Labor, in the "Great Strike" of 1917.

In May 1917, in another surprise, Meagher was appointed to the Legislative Council. This was the Upper House of State Parliament, able to reject the legislation of the Legislative

Assembly – and usually containing a majority of conservatives. It was not an elected body, as was the Legislative Assembly, but a body of members nominated by the state Governor on the recommendation of the current government. After an initial appointment of five years, members could be appointed for life.

Also in May, he made a sixth application for re-instatement before the three-member Full Court, headed by Chief Justice Sir William Cullen. Meagher argued that in the twenty-one years since being struck off, and since his last application 1909, he had shown conduct that justified re-instatement. The barrister representing the Law Institute argued against the application on the grounds of the Dean Case and Meagher's "complicity in the Willis land frauds".[8] The application was refused.

In November 1919, Meagher made a seventh application. He asked the Chief Justice, Sir William Cullen, to recuse himself from the hearing as he had, over the years, shown a bias towards him – the Chief Justice had refused to meet him in his role as Lord Mayor and, on several occasions, had told officials he would not attend a function if Meagher would be on the same platform. The Chief Justice declined. Meagher also outlined a number cases where solicitors had been struck off for serious legal offences, but were later reinstated after ten years or less – one of these had served two years in gaol and was re-instated after seven years. Again his application was refused.[9]

Dick Meagher resigned from the Legislative Council and contested the state election in March 1920 but lost. He published a book, titled *A Twenty-Five Years Battle* and subtitled *Still Fighting On*, in which he provided the speeches and evidence he gave to the 1919 Full Court, with additional material. In December, the Legislative Assembly passed a most extraordinary bill titled the Legal Practitioner Amendment

Epilogue

bill by 30 votes to 9 – the express purpose of which was to re-instate Meagher as a solicitor.[10] The bill, which featured an impassioned speech by Sir Joseph Carruthers in its favour, was passed by the conservative Legislative Council by just five votes, 24 -19. After twenty-five years, Dick Meagher was finally re-instated albeit by an act of parliament. Newspapers editorialised against the principle of Parliament overriding the Full Court.

On January 7, 1921, Dick Meagher made his first court appearance defending a client at Central Criminal Court. From here Meagher prospered and never looked back, later forming a profitable legal partnership with Richard Sproule.

Dick Meagher had married Alice Osmond in January 1891. She was four years older than him and throughout the marriage he was devoted to her – the marriage was childless. Alice received high praise in her role of Lady Mayoress. But she always had a fragility of health, and in her final years was an invalid. She died in 1924. Meagher donated land, adjacent to their country resort in Lawson, Blue Mountains, for the erection of a Catholic church in her honour. In 1929, the Catholic Church conferred a Papal Knighthood on him.

Richard Denis Meagher died in 1931 at the age of sixty-five. He left a large estate of £32,000 (roughly worth nearly a million dollars today), of which £20,000 went to the Catholic Church. One of the minor beneficiaries was Daniel Green.

While there was a hard core of the conservative legal fraternity, who never forgave him the Dean affair, Dick Meagher had more than redeemed himself in the eyes of the general population.

Daniel Green may have been banished from the Crick legal offices in 1895, but six years later he worked closely

Character on Trial

After Richard Meagher was re-elected Lord Mayor in December 1916, this newspaper cartoon appeared following the announcement that the mayoral allowance would be increased from £1,000 to £1,500.

with Paddy Crick on the Coningham Case, and once again some of his actions were rather dubious – he has been described as having a "mania for mischief".[11]

In November 1900, Arthur Coningham sued his wife Alice for divorce on the grounds of her adultery with Father Dr Denis O'Haran, private secretary to Cardinal Patrick Moran at St Mary's Cathedral, Sydney. Coningham had originally demanded £5,000 compensation from the Catholic Church, but the Cardinal refused on the basis of O'Haran's fervent denials of any sexual relations with Alice Coningham. O'Haran was a physically attractive man and, on this basis alone, rumours had previously circulated of indiscretions by him. Arthur, a noted cricketer who had played one test match against England, currently operated a chemist shop. He was a lapsed Protestant but Alice was Catholic and a regular attendee at St Mary's. Alice claimed that O'Haran was the father of the third Coningham child, not Arthur.

Before the trial could get under way, Fr O'Haran charged solicitor Ernest Abigail – representing Coningham – with attempting to coerce Thomas Coogan to give a false statement in the case. Abigail was committed to trial but the case was later dismissed by the Full Court (as a one-on-one situation). The

Epilogue

civil trial opened the next day with John Want representing the Church (at a fee of over £2,000) and solicitor H A Moss representing Coningham. Cross-examining Alice, Want soon established that following Arthur's discovery of her infidelities, they were still co-habiting. This caused Moss to withdraw as Coningham's solicitor, and Arthur conducted the case himself (very capably).

A schismatic controversy led by Rev William Dill-Macky (a high profile Presbyterian minister) opened up, both in and out of court, attacking Catholic practices. It was falsely suggested, for example, that Fr O'Haran could have sinful relations with a woman, go to confession the next day to be forgiven his sins, then lie about it with a clear conscience in court i.e. evidence given in court by Catholics could not be trusted. Catholics complained that the jury were all Protestants; that the Judge was Protestant and showing his bias. In the end, the jury could not agree and a new trial was ordered.

For the second trial in March 1901, Paddy Crick, himself a staunch Catholic, was engaged to represent the Catholic Church, and Daniel Green, also Catholic, became his secret assistant. The only evidence of adultery were the dates of her trysts with Fr O'Haran, which Alice Coningham supplied to the court – and each of these was a time when O'Haran said he was alone. Crick believed that someone inside the Catholic Church was supplying the dates to Coningham, knowing when he was alone, and soon established this to be the case – it was one of O'Haran's fellow priests, who had a complete hatred of him.

In giving the dates to Coningham, the treacherous priest signed himself "Zero". Green began a secret correspondence with Alice, posing as Zero, and supplying her with two dates that he knew O'Haran could establish his presence elsewhere. Alice had a cab

Character on Trial

Arthur Coningham, left, was a chemist and a first class cricketer having played one test match for Australia. Father Denis O'Haran, right, was envied by some of his fellow priests due to his favoured position with Cardinal Moran.

driver who was willing to swear he drove her to O'Haran at any time she claimed. She told the Judge that she had been mistaken in the tryst dates she gave in the first trial, and then supplied the Court with the new dates given to her by Green (as Zero). O'Haran was then able to deny these purported assignations as he was attending public functions on these dates with many witnesses present. Alice had been staying at a boarding house after separating from Arthur. Green bought the boarding house, and was able at some stage to enter her room and steal some of her correspondence. Crick then produced these incriminating letters in court and read them out. There could be no doubt of Father O'Haran's innocence, and the divorce case was dismissed with O'Haran completely cleared of any wrong.[12]

Green subsequently wrote and published a book called "The Secret History of the Coningham Case" under the pseudonym of "Zero". The Coninghams were not charged with any offence and moved to New Zealand.

Daniel opened a betting shop in 1904, but following a change of law and several police raids, faced insolvency. He soon recovered and became a backer of many causes during the rest of his life – more often than not, preferring to be in the background. He was a cultured bachelor interested in theatre, literature, art. A keen supporter of the Labor Party, but not a member, he strongly campaigned against conscription during World War I. He was always a friend of the poor, and not only financially – visitors to his house would often find poor people there receiving some care from him.[13]

Daniel died in 1939 at the age of seventy with his estate owing £5,000.

With time off for good behaviour, George Dean served just over nine years of his fourteen-year sentence. Newspapers carried the story that George was due to be released at six o'clock on the morning of Friday, December 9, 1904. At this time, about 250 people[14] had gathered outside the gates of Darlinghurst Gaol not realising that, shortly after his incarceration, he had been transferred to Goulburn Gaol (a gaol for "first timers"). In the three months before his release, George was permitted to let his hair grow and to grow a beard – there were now streaks of grey in his hair. As he no longer possessed any civilian clothes, a set of clothes was given to him. He was also given about £20 as money earned from his work in the gaol (three pennies per week in the first year, then one shilling per week in succeeding years). There had also been newspaper talk as to his future – a lecture tour was commonly speculated. Daniel Green, representing some group, had gone to Goulburn the day before his release, met with George and offered him some scheme which did not enthuse George.¹⁵

Anticipating that a large crowd, including the press, would be waiting for George, the Gaol authorities released him six hours early, at midnight. A Gaol official walked the two miles to Goulburn Railway Station with him, bought a second-class ticket to Sydney, and saw him off on the train departing at 1:00 am. Green was one of the many disappointed people at the non-appearance of George through the gaol gate at six o'clock.

The *Evening News* noted: "The liberated man was dressed in a plain dark suit, and wore a small chocolate coloured soft felt hat, with a concave crown, the hat being a full size too small for him. He still wears a moustache, and has also grown a short beard of dark colour. Apparently he is thinner than when before the court … On taking his seat in the railway carriage, Dean was evidently anxious to avoid observation. He spread a newspaper out before him, as though with the intention of reading, and held it well before his face … There were a large number of people on the platform to witness the departure of the mail [train], but few were aware of Dean's identity, while scarcely any were certain of it … In prison Dean is said to have been very well behaved. On his release, a moderate sum of money was paid to him, being the amount paid to prisoners for their labour."¹⁶

The *News* was the only newspaper to meet George's train at Central Station at 6:00 am (apparently warned by their Goulburn reporter). The reporter approached George with some innocuous banter after which George said sternly: "Now, tell me, what is it you want with me? I know you are after something."

Epilogue

"To be candid I believe you are George Dean, and I would like to have a chat with you."

"Yes I am George Dean. I won't deny it."

The reporter introduced himself as being from the *Evening News*. George resented the intrusion, but following assurances from the reporter that he was not there to "injure him" or "make matters more difficult", he relented.

"I have served my sentence," George said, "and now all I ask is to be left alone, and not be interfered with."

"Did they treat you kindly there?" the reporter ventured.

"Oh, yes. Well, I won't say kindly. They treated me fairly. They were just, for I was a man amenable to the rules of the prison, and never gave them trouble."

"What were you principally engaged at in the prison?"

"I spent a good deal of my time in the machinery-room, connected with the electric lighting, but I have been engaged at other employment there too … I can get plenty of employment, and I will have no trouble on that score. I have plenty of friends here, but I don't want a fuss made over me … I served my time and bore my punishment like a man, and now I want to be left alone, and I intend to get my living honestly and respectably."

The *News* noted: "Just at that instant a tramway water sprinkler came up, and … the driver – a great big fellow – jumped off, and said with a shout, "Hallo George, is that you?" and [with] his hand outstretched, rushed up to Dean and greeted him with a warmth that left no doubt of his friendly feelings. Dean quickly recognised his friend, and returned the greeting, and a number of friendly inquiries were exchanged … Then Dean, with a parting handshake with his friend, and a friendly nod to the reporter, ran across the roadway, and was soon speeding on his way home."

The *News* also noted that unlike his first prison release in 1895 – to rapturous applause and back slapping – George was very keen to stay well out of the limelight this time. The *News* was unexpectedly impressed with the way he spoke, his command of language.

Reports stated that George went to friends at Camperdown (Konnecke probably). He initially returned to work on ferries, but not with Captain Summerbell who had died in 1900. Within a few years, George moved to the Hay district where he would spend the rest of his life working as a mechanic.

George Dean died on May 7, 1933, in the Hay District Hospital, following his admission suffering heart trouble. He was sixty-five. He had lived in the Hay district for over twenty-five years and was described as "highly esteemed" at the time of his death.[17] His death certificate[18] recorded his name as "Arthur George Dean", suggesting he may have used the name of "Arthur Dean" on arrival there, attempting to circumvent knowledge of his criminal past. But Hay residents certainly knew him as *the* George Dean. Newspapers throughout Australia recorded his death and recalled the infamous events of 1895.

The *Riverina Recorder* stated:[19] "Those who had dealings with him in that [Hay] district had nothing but good to say of him, and the notorious poisoning case of 1895 was almost forgotten when his death brought it into prominence again."

The *Riverine Grazier*, Hay's local newspaper, briefly mentioned his criminal past, and included the following in his obituary:[20] "George Dean came to this district to follow his occupation of mechanical engineer, and he was first employed at *Canoon*, by the then holders of the station. Afterwards he

Epilogue

did similar work at *Toogimbie, Benduck* and other pastoral holdings, his last contracts being on *Tupra*. He was a reliable and most proficient worker, and there was nothing about engines, electrical appliances or motor cars which he did not know. His services were much in demand, and he was never idle. All those who engaged him spoke well of him, and of his work. He was well educated, was well read, and was rather an entertaining conversationalist. He made many friends in this district and in other parts of the State in which he travelled. Although for over a quarter of a century the Hay district had been his headquarters, he was often asked to go to other districts to carry out work of a technical character on engines and machinery."

The brevity of his will, just six lines, was also noted by newspapers. George left a substantial sum of £2,223 (roughly worth $75,000 today) to his unmarried daughter, Florence, then aged thirty-eight. And one has to wonder: in all of those years since Florence was a baby in 1895, had George ever seen or been in contact with her? What were her thoughts about him, the father who tried to murder her mother?

During the conspiracy trial, George wrote some doggerel verse and handed it to his lawyer, Colonna Close. One such verse was headed *Cruel*:[21]

> *First, I am sentenced to death;*
> *Secondly, I am commuted to penial [sic] servitude for life;*
> *Thirdly, I am released and a free pardon is given me;*
> *Fourthly, I am arrested for conspiracy;*
> *Fifthly, for making a false statement;*
> *And finally winds up with 14 years' P.S. [Penal Servitude]*

While this did reflect a certain amount of his current anxiety, it was complete self-absorption – there had never been any sign of regret (other than he was caught) of his cruelty to Mary.

How could such positive obituaries be written about him? Had George achieved some degree of redemption? How could this man – ever so popular and respected by so many people – have ever thought to poison his wife, the mother of his baby, within twelve months of marriage, wanting her dead, and causing her so much physical and mental pain?

So much darkness flowed beneath the placid surface of George Dean.

REFERENCES AND NOTES

Bibliography

Allen, Sir Carleton Kemp, *Aspects of Justice*, Steven & Sons, London, 1958.

Australian Medical Journal, The Dean Case, July 1895.

Blackwell, Leslie, *Death Cell at Darlinghurst*, Victoria, Hutchinson, 1970.

Clune, Frank, *Scandals of Sydney Town*, Angus & Robertson, Sydney, 1957.

Higgins, J F (Editor), *Vindication The Celebrated Dean Case*, self-published, Sydney, C. 1910

Jacobs, Philip *A Famous Australian Trials and memories of the Law*, Robertson & Mullens, Melbourne, 1942.

Meagher, Richard, *A Twenty Years' Battle*, William Brooks & Co, Sydney, 1920.

Pearl, Cyril, *Wild Men of Sydney*, W H Allen, London, 1958.

Stoljar, Jeremy, *The Australian Book of Great Trials*, Murdock Books Australia, Sydney, 2011

Woods, G D, *A History of Criminal Law in New South Wales, The Colonial Period 1788-1900*, Federation Press, Sydney, 2002

"Zero" pseudonym of Green, Daniel, *The Secret History of the Coningham Case*, self-published, Sydney, 1901

Lennan, Jo & Williams, George, *The Death Penalty in Australian Law*, Sydney Law Review, 2012, Vol 34, p.659-94

REFERENCES AND NOTES

Abbreviations

AONSW – Archives Office of New South Wales
AONSW-SB – AONSW Special Bundle
AS – *Australian Star* (newspaper)
BDM – Birth, Death and Marriage
DRC – Dean Royal Commission Report
DT – *Daily Telegraph* (newspaper)
EN – *Evening News* (newspaper)
GD – George Dean
SMH – *Sydney Morning Herald* (newspaper)

All dates are 1889 unless otherwise stated.

Prologue: Ernst Büttner on Trial

1. *AS*, Mar 19 p.5, Mar 20 p.5; *EN*, Mar 20 p.5,6; *SMH*, Mar 21 p.5
2. *EN*, April 30 p.8; *AS*, April 30 p.4,6
3. *EN*, May 9 p.8
4. *SMH*, May 10 p.3
5. *Brisbane Courier*, May 11 p.6
6. *AS*, May 13 p.5
7. *AS*, May 14 p.6
8. *SMH*, May 14 p.5
9. *SMH*, May 15 p.8
10. *EN*, May 14 p.4
11. *AS*, May 16 p.5
12. *AS*, May 17 p.4
13. *EN*, May 17 p.3
14. *Maitland Mercury*, May 21 p.4
15. *Bulletin*, May 18
16. *AS*, May 18 p.4,6
17. *Australasian Medical Gazette*, June 15 p.244- 245
18. *AS*, May 29 p.5
19. Clune p.72
20. *Newcastle Morning Herald*, May 1 p.6
21. Clune p.74
22. *SMH*, July 24 p.11

All dates are 1895 unless otherwise stated.

Chapter 1 First Wedding Anniversary

1. *SMH*, Apr 20 p.6 1891
2. Summerbell, DRC Q1417-1445
3. NSW BDM M#1894/433
4. Elliott, DRC Q8403-8415
5. Brennan, Dean Committal Deposition.
6. The Dean marriage date is

REFERENCES AND NOTES

often given as March 9 rather than March 8, and the date of arrest is usually given as March 9, the date of Dean's first appearance in court, rather than March 8, his arrest date. Both March 9 dates appeared in Windeyer's Judge's Notes.

7. *Brisbane Courier*, Oct 18. The letter is a copy with the spelling corrected.
8. *Brisbane Courier*, Oct 18 & AONSW 9/6896-97. Here the *Courier* version is printed with its corrected spelling.

Chapter 2 Committal

1. *AS*, Mar 19 p.5
2. *AS*, Mar 19 p.6
3. DRC p.33-42. The testimony of Mary Dean and other witnesses is taken from the depositions taken at the committal hearing. It is supplemented by reports from the newspapers, particularly the Australian Star and the *Daily Telegraph*, which give many of the questions rather than just the answers as in the depositions.
4. *DT*, Mar 22

5. DRC Depositions p.37
6. *AS*, Mar 22 p.7; *DT*, Mar 22
7. *SMH* Mar 22 p.3
8. DRC Depositions p.40
9. *AS*, Mar 25 p.6

Chapter 3 The Hanging Judge

1. Woods p.409
2. Woods p.389
3. *SMH*, Oct 22, 1888 p.7
4. *Bulletin*, Nov 1, Dean Case p.5
5. Woods p.408
6. *AS*, April 4 p.5
7. *SMH*, April 5 p.6
8. DRC Judge's notes. There were no trial depositions. Only the Judge's notes served as the official record (and one wonders how a judge, such as Windeyer, maintained them in sessions that lasted in excess of 12 hours). This chapter depends heavily on the Judge's Notes recorded by Windeyer. They are supplemented by newspaper reports, but these tended to give brief summaries of the proceeding generally, but greater detail in certain parts. The lengthy daily court sittings contributed to this newspaper inconsistency

257

REFERENCES AND NOTES

of detail, whereas the committal hearing kept to daylight hours.
9. DRC Judge's notes p.23
10. *SMH*, Apr 5 p.6
11. DMC Judge's Notes p.24
12. *Sunday Times*, April 21 p.5
13. *AS*, April 5 p.5
14. R v Kops, NSW Law Report 14, 1893
15. *AS*, April 6 p.3
16. *Bulletin*, Nov 1 Dean Case p.4
17. DRC Judge's Notes p.32
18. *SMH*, April 8 p.6; *EN*, April 6 p.5
19. *AS*, April 8 p.6
20. *AS*, April 8 p.3
21. *AS*, April 8 p.3

Chapter 4 An Innocent Man

1. *DT*, April 10 p.6
2. *AS*, April 10 p.5
3. *EN*, April 9 p.5
4. *DT*, April 10 p.4
5. *The Age*, April 10 p.4
6. *Australian Workman*, April 13 p.2
7. *Truth*, April 14 p.1
8. *Bulletin*, April 13 p.6
9. *DT*, April 17 p.5
10. *AS*, April 17 p.5; meeting p.1
11. *DT*, April 18 p.6
12. *AS*, April 10 p.5
13. *DT*, April 17 p.5
14. *EN*, April 11 p.6; *Sunday Times*, April 14 p.5
15. *Sunday Times*, April 14 p.5
16. *Sunday Times*, April 14 p.5
17. *EN*, April 18 p.4
18. AONSW-SB 5-7744.1
19. *DT*, April 18 p.6
20. *EN*, April 17 p.4
21. Woods p.253-254
22. *DT*, April 18 p.5
23. *Hansard* 1895 p.5340-5361
24. *SMH*, April 18 p.5
25. *DT*, April 23 p.5
26. *EN*, April 23 p.6
27. *DT*, April 18 p.4
28. *Truth*, April 21 p.1
29. *AS*, April 18 p.4
30. *SMH*, April 18 p.4
31. *DT*, April 27 p.6
32. *SMH*, April 30 p.5
33. *AS*, April 30 p.3
34. *Sunday Times*, April 25 p.5
35. *DT*, April 25 p.6

Chapter 5 The Secret Wedding

1. *AS*, Oct 12 p.5
2. *DT*, Oct 12 p.5
3. Victoria BDM M-1865 #38,

REFERENCES AND NOTES

      B-1865 #23881; NSW BDM
B-1867 #05173, B-1869
#05518, D-1869 #02526
4. *DT*, Oct 12 p.5
5. *SMH*, May 14 p.5
6. *AS*, May 14 p.6
7. DRC p.54
8. *Truth*, May 5 p.7
9. *DT*, Oct 10 p.6
10. *AS*, Oct 10 p.5
11. NSW BDM M-1894 #00433
12. DRC p.48-50
13. *Truth*, May 12 p.5
14. DRC p.67
15. DRC p.244-246
16. DRC p.249
17. DRC p.67
18. DRC p.48-51
19. Committal depositions DRC p.37; *Truth*, May 5 p.7 This is the only source for the loss of £62.
20. DRC p.232
21. *Truth*, May 5 p.7

Chapter 6 Pickpockets and Thieves

1. *DT*, May 14 p.3
2. *AS*, May 15, 1895 p.5
3. www.oldbaileyonline.org
4. The Argus, Nov 20, 1873 p.9
5. The Argus, May 1, 1874 p.6; The Age, Feb 14, 1879 p.3
6. The Age, Feb 14, 1877 p.7
7. Truth, June 2 p.1
8. DT, May 16 p.3
9. DRC p.2
10. *DT*, May 16 p.3 Exchanges between barristers Salomons and Pilcher appeared in newspapers but were not recorded in the official transcripts.
11. DRC p.11
12. DRC p.17
13. DRC p.63-66
14. *DT*, May 21 p.3
15. DRC p.57-63
16. *DT*, May 21 p.3
17. Some of Asbury's details were inexact. He married in 1853, not 1854; his wife arrived on the ship *Sir Robert Seppings* not the *Sir Robert Devon*; etc.
18. *Truth*, May 26 p.1
19. DRC p.70-77
20. *Truth*, May 19 p.4
21. DRC p.176
22. DRC p.6-10
23. DRC p.84-91
24. DRC p.233-249
25. DRC p.171-173
26. DRC p.241-242
27. DRC p.181

REFERENCES AND NOTES

28. *AS*, June 6 p.5
29. *SMH*, June 7 p.5

Chapter 7 Neighbours
1. DRC; Dr Martin's report – appendix to DRC
2. DRC p.119-124, p.124-126, p.126-127
3. DRC p.187-189
4. DRC p.121
5. DRC p.127-129
6. DRC p.95
7. DRC p.96
8. DRC p.77-81
9. DRC p.132-133
10. DRC p.134-135
11. DRC p.141-142
12. DRC p.179-180
13. DRC p.235
14. DRC p.237-238
15. DRC p.146-153
16. DRC p.237
17. DRC p.270
18. *DT*, June 27 p.3

Chapter 8 Justice Demands
1. *Australian Medical Journal*, July 20, 1895 p.321-324
2. *AS*, June 29 p.5
3. *EN*, June 29 p.6
4. *DT*, June 29 p.5
5. *EN*, July 2 p.1; *DT*, July 2 p.3
6. *EN*, July 3 p.4
7. *EN*, July 5 p.8
8. *Weekly Times*, Oct 19 p.22
9. *SMH*, Oct 10 p.5
10. *AS*, July 3 p.8
11. DRC p.147
12. *Australian Workman*, Sep 21 p.2
13. *AS*, Sep 17 p.5
14. *AS*, Sep 18 p.6
15. *Bulletin*, July 6

Chapter 9 A Bruised Ego
1. *DT*, July 16 p.5
2. *Newcastle Morning Herald*, July 19 p.5
3. *EN*, Aug 10 p.4; Sep 4 p.3; Oct 1 p.6
4. *Hansard*, 1895 p.896
5. *Hansard*, 1895 p.972
6. *Sunday Times*, Sep 22 p.5
7. *EN*, Sep 25 p.5
8. *Hansard*, 1895 p.1082
9. *Hansard*, 1895 p.1151-1154
10. *AS*, Sep 27 p.5
11. *Sunday Times*, Sep 29 p.9
12. *AS*, Sep 30 p.5
13. *National Advocate*, Oct 1 p.2
14. *EN*, Oct 1 p.6
15. *Hansard*, 1895 p.1242-1253
16. *Hansard*, 1895 p.1286-1298

REFERENCES AND NOTES

17. *Hansard*, 1895 p.1298-1317
18. *Sunday Times*, Oct 6 p.5
19. *Truth*, Oct 6 p.5
20. *Hansard*, 1895 p.1482-1488
21. *DT*, Oct 9 p.3
22. *SMH*, Oct 10 p.5; *DT*, Oct 10 p.5; *AS*, Oct 10 p.2
23. *AS*, Oct 10 p.5

Chapter 10 Perjury

1. *DT*, Oct 10 p.5
2. *SMH*, Oct 10 p.5
3. *DT*, Oct 10 p.5
4. *EN*, Oct 12 p.4
5. *AS*, Oct 11 p.6
6. *AS*, Oct 21 p.5
7. *EN*, Oct 18 p.4
8. *SMH*, Oct 19 p.10
9. *AS*, Oct 24 p.6
10. *EN*, Oct 23 p.4; Oct 23 p.5
11. *SMH*, Oct 25 p.5-6
12. *DT*, Oct 26 p.10
13. *AS*, Oct 26 p.5

Chapter 11 Conspiracy

1. *AS*, Oct 31 p.6
2. *AS*, Nov 1 p.6
3. *DT*, Oct 31 p.6; Nov 8 p.3
4. *AS*, Nov 1 p.6
5. *AS*, Oct 10, 1895 p.7; *DT*, Oct 10, 1895 p.3
6. *AS*, Nov 12, 1895 p.5; *DT*, Nov 13, 1895 p.3
7. *AS*, Nov 13, 1895 p.5
8. *Truth*, Dec 15, p.5
9. *DT*, Dec 3, 1895 p.6
10. *EN*, May 11, 1892 p.6
11. *DT*, Dec 10 p.3
12. *DT*, Dec 11 p.3
13. *DT*, Dec13 p.3
14. *DT*, Dec14 p.10
15. *AS*, Dec 16 p.5
16. *AS*, Dec 16 p.5; *DT*, Dec 16 p.2
17. *Australian Workman*, Dec 28 p.2

Chapter 12 The Scales of Justice

1. *DT*, May 14, 1896 p.3
2. *AS*, May 16, 1896 p.11
3. *SMH*, May 15, 1896 p.3
4. *EN*, May 16, 1896 p.6
5. *EN*, May 16, 1896 p.6
6. *AS*, June 1, 1896 p.5; June 2, 1896 p.6
7. *AS*, June 2, 1896 p.6
8. John Mortimer, *The Primrose Path*
9. *DT*, Dec13, 1895 p.3
10. DRC, Depositions p.38-39
11. *Hansard*, 1895 p.1486; *DT*, Nov 1 p.5
12. *Argus*, Oct 19, 1897 p.5
13. *EN*, Oct 19, 1897 p.4

14. *AS*, Oct 14, 1895 p.6
15. *AS*, June 7, 1900 p.4
16. *SMH*, Dec 31, 1921 p.8
17. *DT*, Sep 28, 1895 p.5

20. *Riverine Grazier*, May 9, 1933 p.2
21. *AS*, Nov 30, 1895 p.9

Epilogue: Character on Trial

1. *SMH*, Jan 24, 1907 p.7-8
2. *SMH*, Mar 16, 1907 p.13
3. *AS*, Dec 12, 1906 p.2
4. *AS*, July 29, 1908 p.1
5. *SMH*, Aug 7,8,9,10,24, 1907
6. Cyril Pearl p.39
7. *Truth*, Sep 18, 1898 p.1,5
8. *SMH*, May 29, 1917 p.8
9. *SMH*, Nov 8, 1919 p.13; Meagher, *A Twenty-Five Years Battle*, p.73
10. *SMH*, Dec 11, 1920 p.14
11. *SMH*, July 29, 1939 p.13
12. Ku-ring-gai Historical Society, *Newsletter Vol 34 #11*
13. *Australian Dictionary of Biography*; *SMH*, July 29, 1939 p.13
14. *AS*, Dec 9, 1904 p.4
15. *Truth*, Dec 11, 1904 p.4
16. *EN*, Dec 9, 1904 p.4
17. *Albury Banner*, May 12, 1933 p.2
18. NSW BDM D-1933 #9026
19. *Riverina Recorder*, Sep 2, 1933 p.1

REFERENCES AND NOTES

The Colony of New South Wales at the time of this story used the English pound (Sterling) as currency.

1 shilling = 12 pence or pennies
20 shillings = 1 pound
1 guinea = 1 pound and 1 shilling (or 21 shillings)
1 pound 7 shillings and 6 pence could be written as:
      £1 7s 6d.   or   £1/7/6 or £1 - 7 - 6
      3/- is read as "three shillings"
      3/6 is read as "three shillings and six pence"

In 1966, when Australia decimalised its currency, £1 became $2, and one shilling (or twelve pennies) became ten cents.

In distance: 1 mile = 1.6 km
                  1 foot = 30 cm

ORDER

Who poisoned Mary Dean?
Maurie Garland

ISBN: 9780987639011	Qty	
RRP	AU$26.99	.....
Postage within Australia	AU$5.00	.....
	TOTAL* $_____	
	* All prices include GST	

Name: ....

Address: ....

....

Phone: ....

Email: ....

Payment: [ ] Money Order   [ ] Cheque   [ ] MasterCard   [ ] Visa

Cardholder's Name:...

Credit Card Number: ....

Signature:..

Expiry Date: ....

Allow 7 days for delivery.

Payment to: Marzocco Consultancy (ABN 14 067 257 390)
                 PO Box 452
                 Torquay Victoria 3228
                 Australia

Be Published

Publish through a successful publisher.
Brolga Publishing is represented through:
• National book trade distribution, including sales, marketing & distribution through Simon & Schuster.
• International book trade distribution to:
    - The United Kingdom
    - Sales representation in South East Asia
• Worldwide e-Book distribution

For details and enquiries, contact:
Brolga Publishing Pty Ltd
ABN 46 063 962 443
PO Box 452
Torquay Victoria 3228
Australia

markzocchi@brolgapublishing.com.au
(Email for a catalogue request)

www.ingramcontent.com/pod-product-compliance
Lightning Source LLC
Chambersburg PA
CBHW050554170426
43201CB00011B/1693